One Pot MEALS

100 RECIPES TO FEED FAMILY AND FRIENDS

One Pot Meals

13-Digit ISBN: 978-1-60433-952-9
10-Digit ISBN: 1-60433-952-7

This book may be ordered by mail from the publisher. Please include $5.99 for postage and handling. Please support your local bookseller first!

Books published by Cider Mill Press Book Publishers are available at special discounts for bulk purchases in the United States by corporations, institutions, and other organizations. For more information, please contact the publisher.

Cider Mill Press Book Publishers
"Where good books are ready for press"
PO Box 454
12 Spring Street
Kennebunkport, Maine 04046
Visit us online! www.cidermillpress.com

Typography: Sentinel, Bushcraft, Helvetica Rounded
Photos on Pages 17, 18, 19, 34, 38, 49, 50, 63, 64, 67, 72, 76, 79, 82, 85, 90, 94–95, 97, 98–99, 102, 106, 109, 110, 113, 114, 117, 118, 121, 134, 137, 141, 142, 145, 146, 148–149, 153, 173, 174, 177, 178–179, 181, 182, 185, 189, 190–191, 193, 206, 209, 219, 220, 223, 224, 227, 228, 232 courtesy of Cider Mill Press Book Publishers.
Front cover image © StockFood / für ZS Verlag / Walter, Alexander
All other photos are used under official license from Shutterstock.com
Front Endpaper Image: Chicken Vindaloo, see page 166
Back Endpaper Image: Crab & Okra Soup, see page 104

Printed in China
1 2 3 4 5 6 7 8 9 0
First Edition

One Pot MEALS

100 RECIPES TO FEED FAMILY AND FRIENDS

SHANE HETHERINGTON

CIDER MILL PRESS

BOOK PUBLISHERS

KENNEBUNKPORT, MAINE

Contents

Introduction

The contemporary world conspires against the family cook. Once the considerable demands of the modern workday have been met, there's typically little time and no energy left to run the gauntlet of selecting a meal that will make everyone happy, shopping for the ingredients, and getting the meal prepped. This fearsome prospect is enough to turn what should be places of comfort—the kitchen and dinner table— into areas that induce extreme anxiety.

One Pot Meals is a way to reclaim these spaces, providing cooks the tools they need to bring their lives back into balance and keep the kitchen at the center of the home, where it belongs. Every element is designed to save time and energy, without sacrificing any flavor. Make-ahead staples such as stocks and sauces provide an invaluable head start, both in terms of preparation and quality. Breakfasts like frittatas, huevos rancheros, and creamy slow-cooked lentils make sure everyone's day gets started with a smile. The soups, salads, and entrees take you on a whirlwind tour of cuisines around the globe, reigniting your passion for cooking and ensuring that your family is sitting at the table every night, eagerly awaiting the exquisite innovation that is to be set before them.

While flavor is always paramount in the kitchen, the days of acting like cleanup is not a large part of the enterprise are long past. Even when time and energy aren't in short supply, the last thing anyone wants to do after a memorable meal is dive into a sinkful of dishes. Taking the exhaustion and time constraints that many face into account, there's no denying that cleaning up afterward is another factor in folks wanting to avoid the kitchen. By limiting the preparations to one cooking vessel, the recipes in this book make sure that the aftermath is as painless as possible, cutting down on dishes and allowing you to spend a few more moments at the table, enjoying the meal and your loved ones.

Home cooking is an essential part of a quality life, cutting down on costs, providing control of what you and your loved ones consume, and promoting time spent together. While the harried pace of the world means that it has never been easier to lose sight of this, *One Pot Meals* makes sure that you can always remain focused on what's important.

Staples & Sides

The biggest key to becoming a one-pot specialist is preparation. If you have fundamental components like Chicken Stock (see page 11) and Marinara Sauce (see page 32) made ahead of time you've already taken a giant step toward cutting down on your workload, while also ensuring that the quality of what's coming out of your kitchen doesn't suffer in the slightest. Also included in this chapter are effortless ways to round out a dish, such as Guacamole (see page 28) and Kimchi (see page 48).

Chicken Stock

**YIELD: 8 CUPS • ACTIVE TIME: 20 MINUTES
TOTAL TIME: 6 HOURS**

Shifting from store-bought to homemade stock is the easiest way to lift what comes out of your kitchen.

1 Place the chicken bones in a stockpot and cover with cold water. Bring to a simmer over medium-high heat and use a ladle to skim off any impurities that float to the top. Add the vegetables, thyme, peppercorns, and bay leaf, reduce the heat to low, and simmer for 5 hours, while skimming to remove any impurities that rise to the top.

2 Strain, allow to cool slightly, and transfer to the refrigerator. Leave uncovered and allow to cool completely. Remove layer of fat and cover. The stock will keep in the refrigerator for 3 to 5 days, and in the freezer for up to 3 months.

INGREDIENTS

7 lbs. chicken bones, rinsed

4 cups chopped yellow onions

2 cups chopped carrots

2 cups chopped celery

3 garlic cloves, crushed

3 sprigs of thyme

1 teaspoon black peppercorns

1 bay leaf

Beef Stock

If you want an extra-smooth stock, try using veal bones instead of beef bones.

INGREDIENTS

7 lbs. beef bones, rinsed

4 cups chopped yellow onions

2 cups chopped carrots

2 cups chopped celery

3 garlic cloves, crushed

3 sprigs of thyme

1 teaspoon black peppercorns

1 bay leaf

1 Place the beef bones in a stockpot and cover with cold water. Bring to a simmer over medium-high heat and use a ladle to skim off any impurities that float to the top. Add the vegetables, thyme, peppercorns, and bay leaf, reduce the heat to low, and simmer for 5 hours, while skimming to remove any impurities that rise to the top.

2 Strain, allow to cool slightly, and transfer to the refrigerator. Leave uncovered and allow to cool completely. Remove layer of fat and cover. The stock will keep in the refrigerator for 3 to 5 days, and in the freezer for up to 3 months.

Fish Stock

**YIELD: 6 CUPS • ACTIVE TIME: 20 MINUTES
TOTAL TIME: 4 HOURS**

This flavorful stock is a must for any seafood-based soup if you want to maximize the fresh flavor of the ocean.

1 Place the olive oil in a stockpot and warm over low heat. Add the vegetables and cook until the liquid they release has evaporated. Add the whitefish bodies, the aromatics, the salt, and the water to the pot, raise the heat to high, and bring to a boil. Reduce heat so that the stock simmers and cook for 3 hours, while skimming to remove any impurities that float to the top.

2 Strain the stock through a fine sieve, let it cool slightly, and place in the refrigerator, uncovered, to chill. When the stock is completely cool, remove the fat layer from the top and cover. The stock will keep in the refrigerator for 3 to 5 days, and in the freezer for up to 3 months.

INGREDIENTS

¼ cup olive oil

1 leek, trimmed, rinsed well, and chopped

1 large yellow onion, unpeeled, root cleaned, chopped

2 large carrots, chopped

1 celery stalk, chopped

¾ lb. whitefish bodies

4 sprigs of parsley

3 sprigs of thyme

2 bay leaves

1 teaspoon black peppercorns

1 teaspoon kosher salt

8 cups water

Vegetable Stock

A great way to make use of your vegetable trimmings. Just avoid starchy vegetables such as potatoes, as they will make the stock cloudy.

INGREDIENTS

2 tablespoons olive oil

2 large leeks, trimmed and rinsed well

2 large carrots, peeled and sliced

2 celery stalks, sliced

2 large yellow onions, sliced

3 garlic cloves, unpeeled and smashed

2 sprigs of parsley

2 sprigs of thyme

1 bay leaf

8 cups water

½ teaspoon black peppercorns

Salt, to taste

1 Place the olive oil and the vegetables in a large stockpot and cook over low heat until the liquid the vegetables release has evaporated. This will allow the flavor to become concentrated.

2 Add the garlic, parsley, thyme, bay leaf, water, peppercorns, and salt. Raise the heat to high and bring to a boil. Reduce heat so that the stock simmers and cook for 2 hours, while skimming to remove any impurities that float to the top.

3 Strain through a fine sieve, let the stock cool slightly, and place in the refrigerator, uncovered, to chill. Remove the fat layer and cover. The stock will keep in the refrigerator for 3 to 5 days, and in the freezer for up to 3 months.

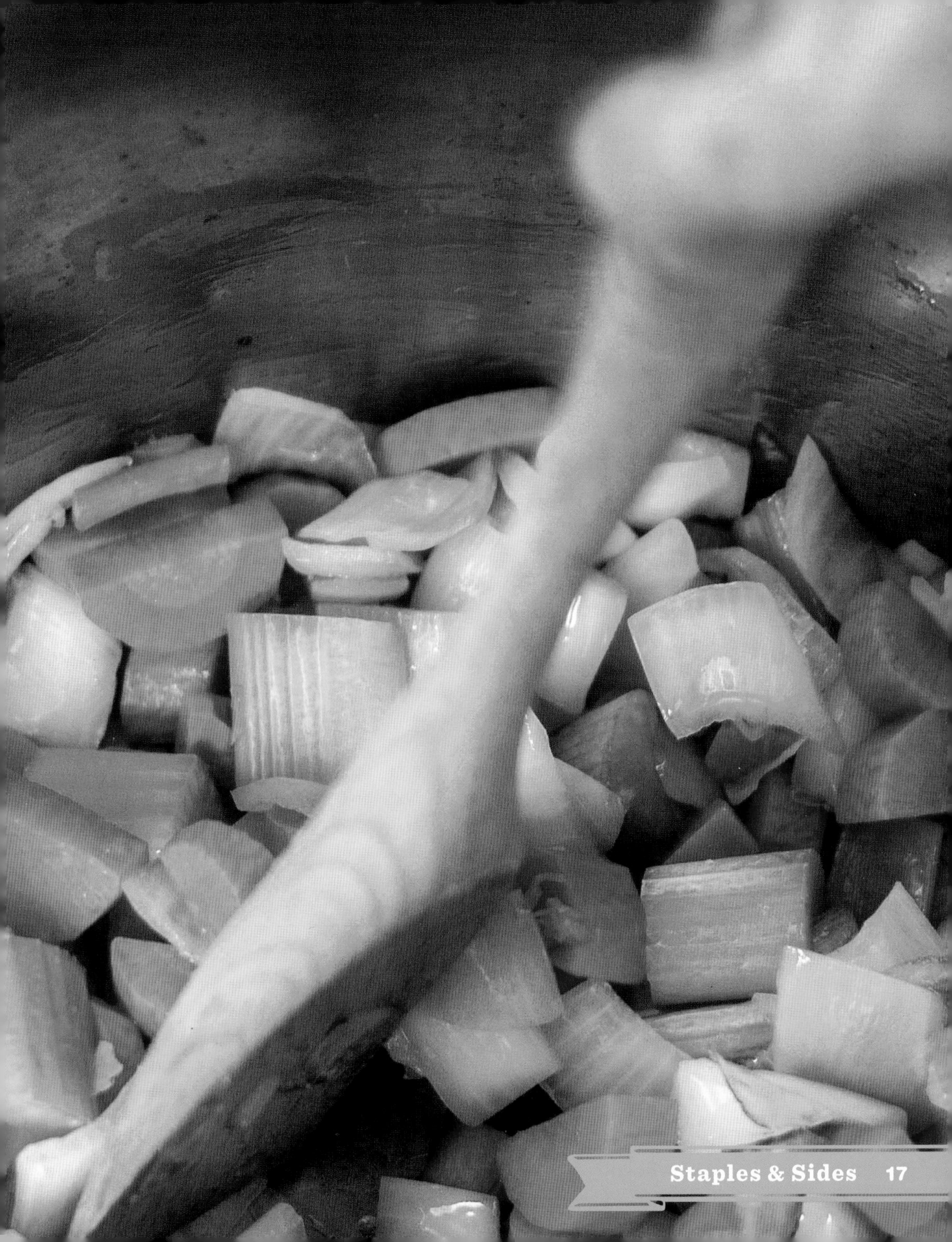

Dashi Broth

YIELD: 6 CUPS • ACTIVE TIME: 10 MINUTES
TOTAL TIME: 1 HOUR

The base of the miso soup that is a cornerstone in Japanese homes, this broth can be used to add a unique briny element to any dish.

1 Place the water and the kombu in a saucepan. Soak for 20 minutes, remove the kombu, and score it gently with a knife.

2 Return the kombu to the saucepan and bring the water to a boil. Remove the kombu as soon as the water boils, so that the broth doesn't become bitter. Add the bonito flakes and return to a boil. Turn off the heat and let the broth stand.

3 Strain through a fine sieve and chill the stock, uncovered, in the refrigerator. Cover when it has cooled completely and store in the refrigerator for up to 1 week and in the freezer for up to 3 months.

INGREDIENTS

8 cups cold water

2 oz. kombu

1 cup bonito flakes

Pizza Dough

**YIELD: 2 BALLS OF DOUGH • ACTIVE TIME: 30 MINUTES
TOTAL TIME: 2½ HOURS**

Versatile and universally loved, pizza is the busy cook's best friend. This dough makes sure your creation sits on a solid foundation.

INGREDIENTS

2 cups warm water (104 to 112°F)

1 tablespoon active dry yeast

2 tablespoons sugar

1 tablespoon olive oil, plus more as needed

2½ cups "00" or all-purpose flour, plus more for dusting

1 teaspoon kosher salt

1 Place the water, yeast, and sugar in a large mixing bowl and stir gently. Let the mixture sit until it begins to foam, about 7 to 10 minutes.

2 Add the olive oil to the mixture and stir. Add the flour and salt and work the mixture with your hands until the dough holds together. Remove the dough from the bowl and transfer it to a flour-dusted work surface. Knead the dough until it is smooth and springy, about 10 minutes. Grease a bowl with olive oil, place the dough in the bowl, cover with a kitchen towel, and store in a naturally warm spot for 1½ to 2 hours.

3 Place the dough on a flour-dusted work surface, cut it into two even pieces, and shape each piece into a smooth ball. If making pizza immediately, stretch the balls of dough into 10" rounds. If not using immediately, place in plastic bags and store in the refrigerator for up to 1 day and in the freezer for up to 2 weeks.

Corn Tortillas

Tortillas are easier to make at home than you think, and the results are well worth it.

1 Place the masa harina and salt in a bowl and stir to combine. Slowly add the warm water and oil and stir until they are incorporated and a soft dough forms. The dough should be quite soft but not at all sticky. If it is too dry, add more water. If the dough is too wet, add more masa harina. Wrap the dough in plastic and let it rest at room temperature for 30 minutes. It can also be stored in the refrigerator for up to 24 hours.

2 Warm a cast-iron skillet over medium-high heat. Pinch off a small piece of the dough and roll it into a ball. Place the ball between two pieces of parchment paper or plastic wrap and use a large cookbook (or something of similar weight) to flatten the ball into a thin disk.

3 Place the disk in the skillet and cook until brown spots begin to appear, about 45 seconds. Flip the disk over, cook for 1 minute, and transfer the cooked tortilla to a plate. Cover with a kitchen towel and repeat with the remaining dough.

INGREDIENTS

2 cups masa harina, plus more as needed

½ teaspoon kosher salt

1 cup warm water (105°F), plus more as needed

2 tablespoons vegetable oil

Grilled Tomato Salsa

YIELD: 1 CUP • ACTIVE TIME: 20 MINUTES
TOTAL TIME: 2 HOURS

Roasting tomatoes on the grill brings out their sweet side and makes this salsa good enough to enjoy on its own.

INGREDIENTS

1 lb. tomatoes, cored and halved

½ tablespoon olive oil

Salt and pepper, to taste

2 tablespoons minced yellow onion

½ jalapeño pepper, stemmed, seeded, and minced

1 tablespoon minced fresh cilantro

1 tablespoon fresh lime juice

1 Preheat your gas or charcoal grill to 450°F. Place the tomatoes, olive oil, salt, and pepper in a large bowl and toss to coat. Let stand for 30 minutes.

2 Place the tomatoes, cut-side down, on the grill and cook until they start to char and soften, about 5 minutes. Carefully turn the tomatoes over and cook until they start bubbling, about 5 minutes. Transfer the tomatoes to a bowl and let cool completely.

3 Chop the tomatoes and place them in a bowl with the remaining ingredients. Stir to combine and let stand at room temperature for 45 minutes. Taste, adjust seasoning if necessary, and serve. The salsa will keep in the refrigerator for up to 2 days.

Salsa Verde

The tart and sweet tomatillo is one of the easiest and most delicious ways to add a burst of color to your table.

1 Place the tomatillos and serrano peppers in a large saucepan and cover with water. Bring to a boil and cook until the tomatillos start to lose their bright green color, about 10 minutes.

2 Drain and transfer the tomatillos and peppers to a blender. Add all of the remaining ingredients, except for the cilantro, and puree until smooth. Top with the cilantro and serve. The salsa will keep in the refrigerator for up to 2 days.

INGREDIENTS

6 tomatillos, husked and rinsed

8 serrano peppers, stemmed and seeded to taste

½ yellow onion

2 garlic cloves, minced

Salt, to taste

¼ cup olive oil

Fresh cilantro, chopped, for garnish

Guacamole

YIELD: 2 CUPS • ACTIVE TIME: 5 MINUTES
TOTAL TIME: 5 MINUTES

Use this as an appetizer to keep hanger to a minimum, or as a side to flank any spicy dish.

INGREDIENTS

2 tablespoons minced red onion

Zest and juice of 1 lime

Salt, to taste

1 jalapeño pepper, stemmed, seeded, and minced

Flesh from 3 ripe avocados, chopped

2 tablespoons chopped cilantro

1 plum tomato, cored, seeded, and diced

1 Place the onion, lime zest and juice, salt, and jalapeño in a mixing bowl and stir to combine.

2 Add the avocados and work the mixture with a fork until the desired consistency has been reached. Add the cilantro and tomato, stir to incorporate, and taste. Adjust seasoning if needed and serve immediately.

Basil Pesto

YIELD: 1 CUP • ACTIVE TIME: 25 MINUTES
TOTAL TIME: 25 MINUTES

This simple pesto is always great to have on hand, as it will give you options in a number of preparations.

1 Warm a small skillet over low heat for 1 minute. Add the walnuts and cook, while stirring, until they begin to give off a toasty fragrance, 2 to 3 minutes. Transfer to a plate and let cool completely.

2 Place the garlic, salt, and walnuts in a food processor or blender and pulse until the mixture is a coarse meal. Add the basil and pulse until finely minced. Transfer the mixture to a mixing bowl and add the oil in a thin stream as you quickly whisk it in.

3 Add the cheeses and stir until thoroughly incorporated. The pesto will keep in the refrigerator for up to 4 days and in the freezer for up to 3 months.

INGREDIENTS

¼ cup walnuts

3 garlic cloves

Salt and pepper, to taste

2 cups firmly packed basil leaves

½ cup olive oil

¼ cup grated Parmesan cheese

¼ cup grated Pecorino Sardo cheese

Marinara Sauce

YIELD: 8 CUPS • ACTIVE TIME: 20 MINUTES
TOTAL TIME: 2 HOURS

Having some of this sauce in the freezer means you always have a head start on a quick, delicious dinner.

INGREDIENTS

4 lbs. tomatoes, quartered

1 large yellow onion, sliced

15 garlic cloves, crushed

2 teaspoons minced fresh thyme leaves

2 teaspoons minced fresh oregano

2 tablespoons olive oil

1½ tablespoons kosher salt

1 teaspoon black pepper

2 tablespoons chopped fresh basil

1 tablespoon chopped fresh parsley

1 Place all of the ingredients, except for the basil and parsley, in a Dutch oven and cook, while stirring constantly, over medium heat until the tomatoes release their liquid and begin to break down, about 10 minutes. Reduce the heat to low and cook, while stirring occasionally, for about 1½ hours, or until the flavor is to your liking.

2 Stir in the basil and parsley and season to taste. The sauce will be chunky. If you prefer a smoother texture, transfer the sauce to a blender and puree.

Spicy Baby Carrots

**YIELD: 6 SERVINGS • ACTIVE TIME: 30 MINUTES
TOTAL TIME: 2 HOURS**

This spice blend is similar to what you would find in a barbecue rub, and it works wonderfully with the sweetness of carrots.

1 Preheat the oven to 375°F. Place all of the ingredients in a mixing bowl and toss to coat.

2 Place the carrots in an even layer in a baking dish. Place in the oven and roast until the carrots are tender, about 25 minutes. Remove and let cool slightly before serving.

INGREDIENTS

2 lbs. baby-cut carrots

2 tablespoons olive oil

2 tablespoons kosher salt

1 teaspoon black pepper

2 teaspoons cumin

1 teaspoon ground fennel seeds

1 teaspoon ground coriander

1 teaspoon paprika

2 teaspoons brown sugar

Zucchini Fritters

YIELD: 4 SERVINGS • ACTIVE TIME: 15 MINUTES
TOTAL TIME: 1½ HOURS

Zucchini has a number of wonderful uses, and turning it into fritters is one of the easiest ways to get people excited about it.

1 Line a colander with cheesecloth and grate the zucchini into the colander. Generously sprinkle salt over the zucchini, stir to combine, and let sit for 1 hour. After 1 hour, press down on the zucchini to remove as much liquid from it as you can.

2 Place the zucchini, flour, Parmesan, and egg in a mixing bowl and stir to combine. Use your hands to form handfuls of the mixture into balls and then gently press down on the balls to form them into patties.

3 Place the oil in a cast-iron skillet and warm over medium-high heat. Working in batches, place the patties into the oil, taking care not to crowd the skillet. Cook until golden brown, about 5 minutes. Flip them over and cook for another 5 minutes, until the fritters are also golden brown on that side. Remove from the skillet, transfer to a paper towel–lined plate, and repeat with the remaining patties. When all of the fritters have been cooked, season with salt and pepper and serve.

INGREDIENTS

1½ lbs. zucchini

Salt and pepper, to taste

¼ cup all-purpose flour

¼ cup grated Parmesan cheese

1 egg, beaten

3 tablespoons olive oil

Spanish Potato Tortilla

YIELD: 6 SERVINGS • ACTIVE TIME: 30 MINUTES
TOTAL TIME: 2 HOURS

Hearty, filling, and easy to master, it's good on its own or as a side.

INGREDIENTS

5 large russet potatoes, peeled and sliced thin

1 Spanish onion, peeled and sliced

½ cup vegetable oil, plus more as needed

½ cup olive oil

10 eggs, at room temperature

Large pinch of kosher salt

1 Place the potatoes, onion, vegetable oil, and olive oil in a 12" cast-iron skillet. The potatoes should be submerged in the oil. If not, add more vegetable oil as needed. Bring to a gentle simmer over low heat and cook until the potatoes are tender, about 30 minutes. Remove from heat and let cool slightly.

2 Use a slotted spoon to remove the potatoes and onion from the oil. Reserve the oil. Place the eggs and salt in a large bowl and whisk to combine. Add the potatoes and onion to the eggs.

3 Warm the skillet over high heat. Add ¼ cup of the reserved oil and swirl to coat the bottom and sides of the pan. Pour the egg-and-potato mixture into the pan and stir vigorously to ensure that the mixture does not stick to the sides. Cook for 1 minute and remove from heat. Place the pan over low heat, cover, and cook for 3 minutes.

4 Carefully invert the tortilla onto a large plate. Return it to the skillet, cook for 3 minutes, and then invert it onto the plate. Return it to the skillet and cook for another 3 minutes. Remove the tortilla from the pan and let it rest at room temperature for 1 hour. Slice into wedges and serve.

Garlic & Chili Broccolini

YIELD: 4 SERVINGS • **ACTIVE TIME: 15 MINUTES**
TOTAL TIME: 15 MINUTES

You can make this with broccoli, but the sweeter flavor of broccolini is a better match for the spice.

1 Bring water to a boil in a cast-iron skillet or Dutch oven. Add the broccolini and cook for 30 seconds. Drain and transfer the broccolini to a paper towel–lined plate.

2 Warm the skillet or Dutch oven over medium-high heat and add the olive oil.

3 When the oil starts to shimmer, add the broccolini and cook until well browned. Turn the broccolini over, add the garlic, season with salt and pepper, and toss to combine. When the broccolini is browned all over, add the red pepper flakes and toss to evenly distribute. Transfer to a serving platter, garnish with the toasted almonds, and serve immediately.

INGREDIENTS

½ lb. broccolini, trimmed

¼ cup olive oil

2 garlic cloves, minced

Salt and pepper, to taste

1 teaspoon red pepper flakes

2 tablespoons toasted almonds, for garnish

Awesome Asparagus

YIELD: 4 SERVINGS • ACTIVE TIME: 10 MINUTES
TOTAL TIME: 10 MINUTES

Ready in minutes and packed with flavor, asparagus is the one-pot specialist's best friend.

INGREDIENTS

3 tablespoons olive oil

1 bunch of asparagus, woody ends removed

1 garlic clove, minced

½ teaspoon kosher salt

½ teaspoon black pepper

Lemon wedges, for serving

1 Warm a 12" cast-iron skillet over medium-high heat and then add the olive oil. When the oil starts to shimmer, add the asparagus and cook, while turning frequently, until they are bright green, about 5 minutes.

2 Add the garlic, salt, and pepper, and shake the pan to distribute evenly. Cook the asparagus for another 2 minutes, transfer to a serving platter, and serve with the lemon wedges.

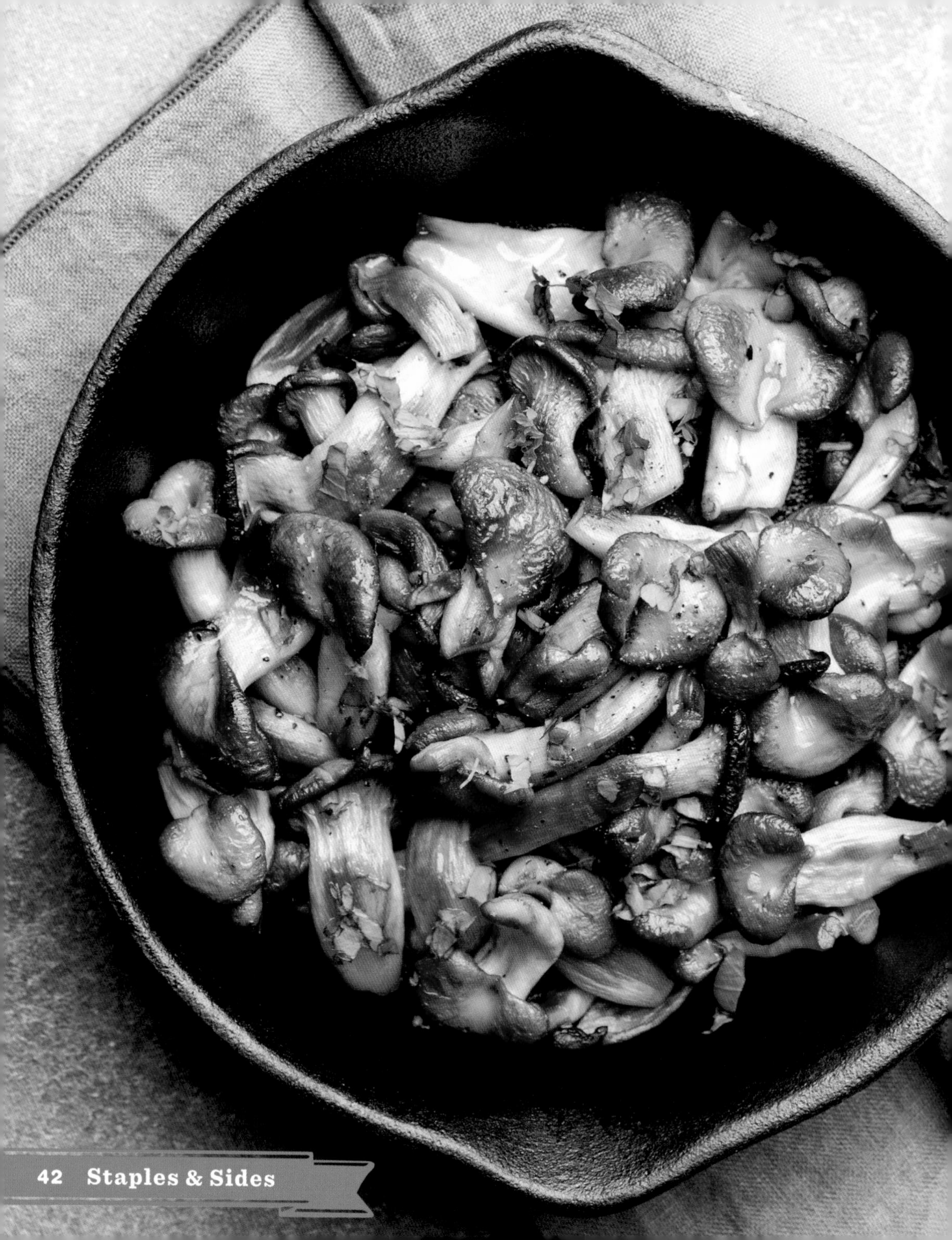

Marvelous Mushrooms

YIELD: 4 SERVINGS • ACTIVE TIME: 20 MINUTES
TOTAL TIME: 30 MINUTES

Cooking mushrooms with lots of butter yields a rich, earthy stew that can work as a side or a topping.

1 Place a 12" cast-iron skillet over medium-high heat and add the butter. When it has melted, add the mushrooms and cook, while stirring, until they begin to soften, about 5 minutes. Reduce the heat to low and simmer, while stirring occasionally, until the liquid the mushrooms released has completely evaporated and they are brown, 15 to 20 minutes.

2 Add the vermouth, season with salt and pepper, and stir to incorporate. Simmer until the mushrooms are very tender and serve immediately.

INGREDIENTS

6 tablespoons unsalted butter, cut into pieces

1 lb. mushrooms, stemmed and sliced

1 teaspoon dry vermouth

Salt and pepper, to taste

Stuffed Tomatoes

YIELD: 6 SERVINGS • ACTIVE TIME: 20 MINUTES
TOTAL TIME: 1 HOUR AND 15 MINUTES

If you want to make these vegetarian, simply swap the sausage out for some toasted and chopped walnuts.

1 Preheat the oven to 375°F. Cut off the tops of the tomatoes and use a spoon to scoop out the insides. Sprinkle salt into the cavities and turn the tomatoes upside down on a paper towel–lined plate. Let stand for about 30 minutes.

2 Warm a 12" cast-iron skillet over medium-high heat and add the sausage, breaking it up with a wooden spoon as it cooks. Cook until there is no pink showing in the meat. When cooked, use a slotted spoon to transfer the sausage to a large bowl and leave the fat in the skillet. Add the onion and garlic to the skillet and cook until the onion is translucent, about 4 minutes. Add the mushrooms and bell pepper and cook over medium heat, while stirring, until they have softened, about 10 minutes. If desired, stir in the red pepper flakes.

3 Add the mushroom mixture, bread crumbs, and sage to the sausage and stir to combine. Season with salt and pepper and fill the tomatoes with the mixture. Sprinkle the Parmesan on top.

4 Wipe out the skillet and place the tomatoes in the pan. Place the stuffed tomatoes in the oven and roast until the tops start to blister and the cheese has melted, about 15 minutes. Remove and serve immediately.

INGREDIENTS

12 small tomatoes

Salt and pepper, to taste

1 lb. sausage, casings removed

1 yellow onion, diced

4 garlic cloves, minced

8 white mushroom caps, diced

½ green bell pepper, stemmed, seeded, and diced

2 teaspoons red pepper flakes (optional)

2 cups plain bread crumbs

2 tablespoons dried sage

1 cup grated Parmesan cheese

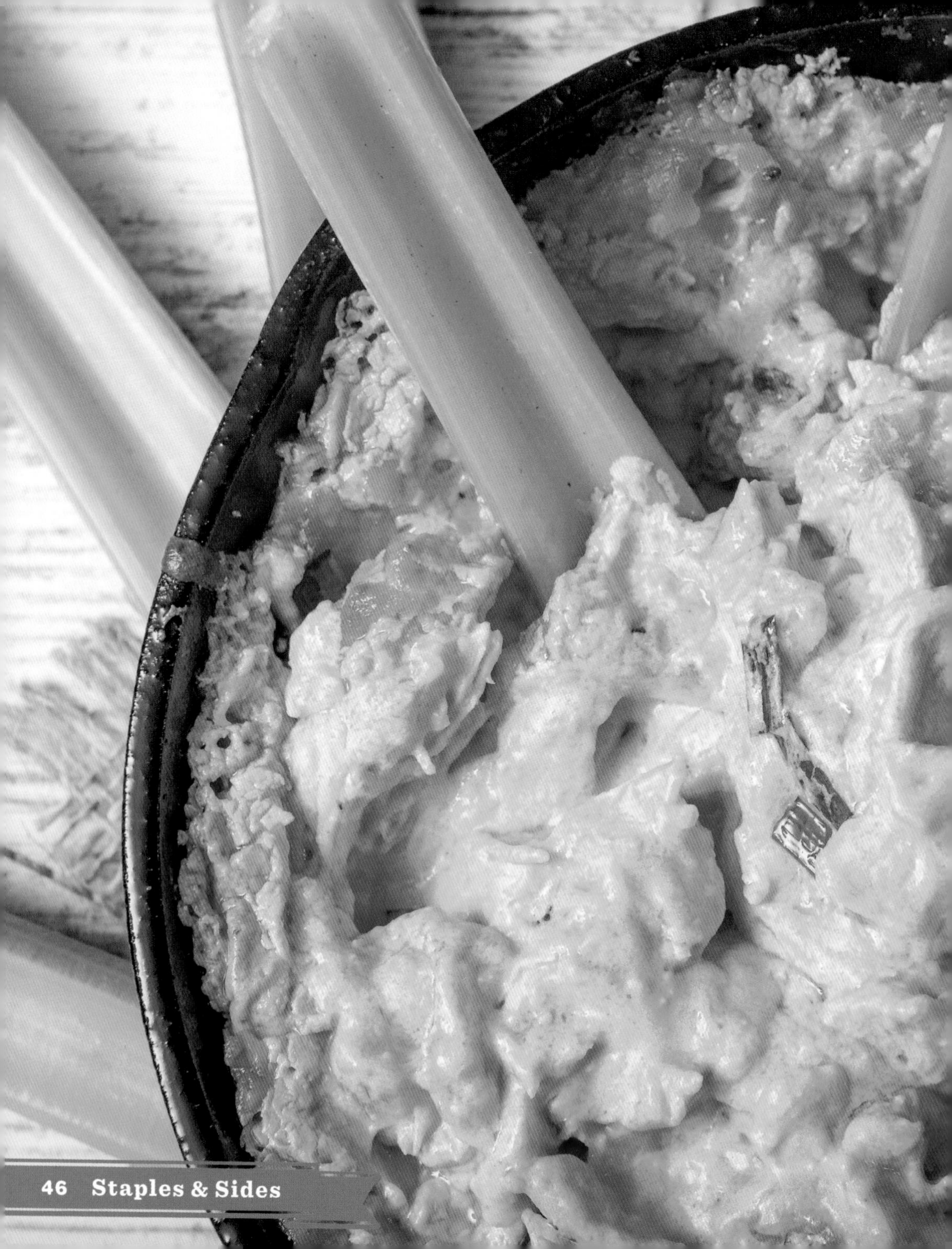

Cheesy Vegetable Dip

**YIELD: 6 SERVINGS • ACTIVE TIME: 20 MINUTES
TOTAL TIME: 1½ HOURS**

The ability to accommodate slices of crusty bread and almost any vegetable makes this dip a godsend in the chaotic swirl of the summer.

1 Place the cream cheese or quark, sour cream, and mozzarella in an oven-safe bowl and stir until well combined. Add the remaining ingredients, stir to combine, and place in the refrigerator for at least 1 hour.

2 Approximately 30 minutes before you are ready to serve the dip, preheat the oven to 350°F.

3 Top the dip with additional mozzarella, place in the oven, and bake until the cheese is melted and slightly brown, about 20 minutes. Remove from the oven and serve immediately.

Note: Quark is a creamy, unripe cheese that is popular in Germany and eastern European countries. If you're intrigued, Vermont Creamery produces a widely available version.

INGREDIENTS

1 cup cream cheese or quark cheese

½ cup sour cream

1 cup shredded mozzarella cheese, plus more for topping

2 tablespoons fresh rosemary leaves, chopped

2 tablespoons fresh thyme leaves, chopped

½ cup diced summer squash

1 cup Swiss chard

1 cup spinach

6 garlic cloves, diced

2 teaspoons kosher salt

1 teaspoon black pepper

Kimchi

**YIELD: 4 CUPS • ACTIVE TIME: 30 MINUTES
TOTAL TIME: 3 TO 7 DAYS**

Simple, flavorful, and versatile, kimchi is the perfect introduction to your new best friend: fermentation.

INGREDIENTS

1 head of Napa cabbage, cut into strips

½ cup kosher salt

2 tablespoons minced ginger

3 garlic cloves, minced

1 teaspoon sugar

5 tablespoons red pepper flakes

3 bunches of scallions, sliced (whites and greens)

Water, as needed

1 Place the cabbage and salt in a large bowl and stir to combine. Wash your hands, or put on gloves, and work the mixture with your hands, squeezing to remove as much liquid as possible from the cabbage. Let the mixture rest for 2 hours.

2 Add the remaining ingredients, work the mixture with your hands until well combined, and squeeze to remove as much liquid as possible.

3 Transfer the mixture to a large mason jar and press down so it is tightly packed together. The liquid should be covering the mixture. If it is not, add water until the mixture is covered.

4 Cover the jar and let the mixture sit at room temperature for 3 to 7 days, removing the lid daily to release the gas that has built up.

Spicy Pickles

A refreshing and delicious preparation that you can confidently bring to the table no matter what else is on it.

1 Place the cucumbers, onion, peppers, and garlic in a large bowl and stir to combine.

2 Place the sugar, apple cider vinegar, mustard seeds, turmeric, and black pepper in a large saucepan and bring to a boil over medium-high heat, while stirring to dissolve the sugar.

3 Add the vegetables and the salt and return to a boil. Remove the pot from heat and let it cool slightly. Fill mason jars with the vegetables and cover with the brine. Let cool completely before sealing and placing in the refrigerator. The pickles will keep in the refrigerator for up to 2 weeks.

INGREDIENTS

1 lb. pickling cucumbers, sliced thin

1 small yellow onion, sliced thin

½ red bell pepper, stemmed, seeded, and sliced thin

1 habanero pepper, stemmed, seeded, and sliced thin

1 garlic clove, sliced

1 cup sugar

1 cup apple cider vinegar

2 teaspoons mustard seeds

½ teaspoon turmeric

Pinch of black pepper

⅓ cup canning & pickling salt

Breakfast

As the crowds outside of every decent greasy spoon prove, we all want to kick the day off with something delicious. But the thought of creating a sinkful of dishes that will be waiting for us when we come home and need to get dinner going keeps many of us from indulging as much as we would like. But no longer. The days of subsisting on stopgaps such as protein bars and store-bought smoothies are in the rearview mirror thanks to the delicious and easy-to-prepare recipes in this chapter.

Bacon & Zucchini Frittata

YIELD: 6 SERVINGS • ACTIVE TIME: 10 MINUTES
TOTAL TIME: 45 MINUTES

It turns out that crisp, salty bacon is the perfect complement to zucchini.

INGREDIENTS

¾ lb. thick-cut bacon, chopped

1 small zucchini, cut into thin rounds

1 garlic clove, minced

4 oz. garlic-herb goat cheese

4 eggs

3 oz. baby spinach

1½ cups half-and-half

½ teaspoon kosher salt

½ teaspoon black pepper

1 Preheat the oven to 350°F. Place the bacon in a 10" cast-iron skillet and cook over medium heat until crispy, about 10 minutes. Transfer the pieces to a paper towel–lined plate. Add the zucchini pieces and garlic to the skillet and cook until the zucchini is just soft, about 6 minutes. Return the pieces of bacon to the skillet, add the goat cheese, and stir until evenly distributed.

2 Whisk the eggs until scrambled. Add the spinach, half-and-half, salt, and pepper, and whisk to combine. Pour the egg mixture into the skillet and shake the skillet to distribute.

3 Put the skillet in the oven and bake until the frittata is puffy and golden brown and the eggs are set, about 35 minutes. Remove from the oven and let the frittata sit for 10 minutes before slicing and serving.

Tamagoyaki

YIELD: 4 SERVINGS • ACTIVE TIME: 15 MINUTES
TOTAL TIME: 15 MINUTES

This is a sweet-and-savory Japanese omelet that takes a bit of practice to get just right. Once you master it, you'll find yourself craving it all the time.

1 Place the eggs, salt, soy sauce, and mirin in a bowl and whisk to combine.

2 Place the olive oil in a 12" cast-iron skillet and warm over medium-high heat. Pour a thin layer of the egg mixture into the pan, tilting and swirling to make sure the egg completely coats the bottom. When the bottom of the egg is just set and there is still liquid on top, use a chopstick to gently roll the egg up into a log. If you overcook the egg, it won't stick as you roll it.

3 When the first roll is at one end of the pan, pour another thin layer of egg mixture into the pan. When the bottom of this layer is set, move the roll back onto it. Roll the layer up to the other end of the pan. Repeat until all of the egg mixture has been used up. Remove the omelet from the pan and let it set for a few minutes before trimming the ends and slicing it into even pieces.

INGREDIENTS

8 large eggs

½ teaspoon kosher salt

2 teaspoons soy sauce

2 tablespoons mirin

1 tablespoon olive oil

Huevos Rancheros

**YIELD: 4 SERVINGS • ACTIVE TIME: 10 MINUTES
TOTAL TIME: 15 MINUTES**

Yet another of the numerous gifts that the Mexican culture has given to the world.

INGREDIENTS

2 tablespoons olive oil

4 corn tortillas (see page 23 for homemade)

1 (14 oz.) can of black beans, drained

1 tablespoon unsalted butter

4 eggs

½ cup grated sharp cheddar cheese

½ cup Cotija or grated Monterey Jack cheese

½ cup salsa (see page 24 or page 27 for homemade), for serving

Jalapeño peppers, sliced, for serving

Fresh cilantro, chopped, for serving

1 Place the oil in a 10" cast-iron skillet and warm over medium-high heat. When the oil starts to shimmer, add the tortillas and cook until they start to brown. Add the beans and butter and mash the beans into the tortillas. Cook until the beans are warmed through, about 4 minutes.

2 Break the eggs over the beans, cover the skillet, and cook until the eggs start to set, about 3 minutes.

3 Remove the lid, top with the cheeses, and serve with salsa, jalapeños, and cilantro.

Ham & Swiss Strata

**YIELD: 4 SERVINGS • ACTIVE TIME: 20 MINUTES
TOTAL TIME: 1 HOUR**

A strata is the ideal way to use up leftovers, or in this case, showcase the flawless combination of ham and Swiss cheese.

1 Place the eggs and milk in a large mixing bowl and whisk to combine. Add the cheese and nutmeg and stir to incorporate. Add the bread pieces, transfer the mixture to the refrigerator, and chill for 30 minutes.

2 Preheat the oven to 400°F. Add the ham, onion, and spinach to the egg-and-bread mixture and stir until evenly distributed. Season with salt and pepper.

3 Coat a 10" cast-iron skillet with the olive oil. Pour in the strata, place the skillet in the oven, and bake until it is golden brown and set in the center, about 25 minutes. Remove from the oven and let cool for 10 minutes before cutting into wedges and serving.

INGREDIENTS

7 eggs, beaten

2 cups whole milk

4 oz. Swiss cheese, shredded

Large pinch of ground nutmeg

3 cups day-old bread pieces

4 oz. ham, diced

1 yellow onion, minced

3 oz. spinach, chopped

Salt and pepper, to taste

2 teaspoons olive oil

Breakfast Tacos

YIELD: 6 SERVINGS • ACTIVE TIME: 10 MINUTES
TOTAL TIME: 1 HOUR

Because tacos are far too good to be limited to the later parts of the day.

1 To prepare the pico de gallo, place all of the ingredients in a mixing bowl and stir to combine. Refrigerate for 1 hour before serving to let the flavors mingle.

2 To prepare the tacos, place the oil in a skillet and warm over medium heat. Place the eggs, seasonings, and cilantro in a mixing bowl and whisk to combine. Add the egg mixture to the skillet and scramble until the eggs are cooked through, 5 to 7 minutes.

3 Serve with the warm tortillas and pico de gallo.

INGREDIENTS
For the Pico de Gallo

4 plum tomatoes, diced

1 jalapeño pepper, stemmed, seeded, and diced

½ cup chopped red onion

¼ cup chopped fresh cilantro

Zest and juice of ½ lime

Salt, to taste

For the Tacos

2 tablespoons olive oil

8 eggs

1 tablespoon chili powder

1 tablespoon cumin

½ tablespoon adobo seasoning

1 tablespoon dried oregano

2 tablespoons chopped fresh cilantro

6 corn tortillas (see page 23 for homemade), warmed

Baked Egg Casserole

YIELD: 6 SERVINGS • ACTIVE TIME: 10 MINUTES
TOTAL TIME: 1 HOUR AND 15 MINUTES

This dish is a great alternative to plain old scrambled eggs.

1 Preheat the oven to 350°F. Place the eggs, water, and half-and-half in a mixing bowl and whisk until combined.

2 Add the remaining ingredients, stir to incorporate, and pour the mixture into a greased square 8" baking dish. Place the dish in the oven and bake until the eggs are set in the middle and a knife inserted into the center comes out dry, about 1 hour. Remove the dish from the oven and let the casserole stand for 5 minutes before serving. Grate additional Parmesan over the top before serving.

INGREDIENTS

12 large eggs

¼ cup water

½ cup half-and-half

3 plum tomatoes, cored and chopped

1 cup chopped spinach

½ cup chopped scallions

1 cup grated Parmesan cheese, plus more for topping

1 tablespoon minced fresh thyme

Salt and pepper, to taste

Peanut Butter & Bacon Oats

YIELD: 6 SERVINGS • ACTIVE TIME: 5 MINUTES
TOTAL TIME: 20 MINUTES

This combination may sound crazy at first, but the salty bacon, crunchy peanut butter, and creamy egg yolk work really well together.

INGREDIENTS

6 slices of thick-cut bacon

6 eggs

2 cups steel-cut oats

6 cups water

1 tablespoon kosher salt

¼ cup crunchy peanut butter

1 Place the bacon in a 12" cast-iron skillet and cook over medium heat until crispy, about 8 minutes. Transfer the bacon to a paper towel–lined plate, add the eggs to the skillet, and fry them in the bacon fat. Transfer the eggs to a plate and tent loosely with aluminum foil to keep warm.

2 Wipe out the skillet, add the oats, water, and salt and cook over medium heat for 7 to 10 minutes, until the oats are tender.

3 While the oats are cooking, chop the bacon. Add the bacon and peanut butter to the oats and stir to incorporate. Ladle the oatmeal into warmed bowls, top each portion with a fried egg, and serve.

Whole Grain Porridge

YIELD: 4 SERVINGS • ACTIVE TIME: 5 MINUTES
TOTAL TIME: 30 MINUTES

Try this recipe as suggested, and then make it your own, swapping in any grain, dried fruit, and milk that you want.

1 Place all of the ingredients, except for the garnishes, in a Dutch oven. Bring to a gentle simmer over medium-low heat and cover. Cook for 20 minutes, stirring occasionally to prevent the porridge from sticking to the bottom of the pot.

2 Remove the porridge from heat and ladle into warm bowls. Peel the apple and grate it over each bowl. Top with the chopped almonds and serve.

INGREDIENTS

1 cup buckwheat groats

1 cup steel-cut oats

2 tablespoons flaxseeds

2 teaspoons cinnamon

1 cup chopped dried fruit (apples, apricots, pineapples, dates, etc.)

2 cups water

2 cups unsweetened almond milk

1 Granny Smith apple, for garnish

¼ cup chopped almonds, for garnish

Grandma Goodrich's Grits

**YIELD: 8 SERVINGS • ACTIVE TIME: 15 MINUTES
TOTAL TIME: 45 MINUTES**

The beauty of cast iron is on full display here, as it lends the bottom a gorgeous burnish.

1 Preheat the oven to 425°F. Place the water in a large cast-iron skillet and bring to a boil. While stirring constantly, slowly add the grits. Cover, reduce the heat to low, and cook, while stirring occasionally, until the grits are quite thick, about 5 minutes. Remove from heat.

2 Place the eggs, 4 tablespoons of the butter, and milk in a bowl, season with salt and pepper, and stir to combine. Stir the cooked grits into the egg mixture, add three-quarters of the cheese, and stir to incorporate.

3 Wipe out the skillet, grease it with the remaining butter, and pour the mixture into the skillet. Place the skillet in the oven and bake for 30 minutes. Remove, sprinkle the remaining cheese on top, and return the grits to the oven. Bake until the cheese is melted and the grits are firm, about 15 minutes. Remove from the oven and let cool slightly before serving.

INGREDIENTS

4 cups water

1 cup quick-cooking grits

2 large eggs

5 tablespoons unsalted butter, at room temperature

¾ cup milk

Salt and pepper, to taste

1 lb. cheddar cheese, grated

Sweet Potato Lentils

YIELD: 6 SERVINGS • ACTIVE TIME: 20 MINUTES
TOTAL TIME: 8 HOURS

Why should oatmeal get to hog the morning spotlight? Lentils are packed with fiber and protein, so you can get a complete meal in one shot.

1 Place all of the ingredients, except for the garnishes, in a slow cooker and stir to combine.

2 Cook on low until the lentils and sweet potatoes have broken down and the mixture is smooth, about 8 hours.

3 Ladle into bowls and garnish with the crushed almonds and cashews.

INGREDIENTS

1 lb. brown lentils, rinsed

2 sweet potatoes, peeled and diced

¾ cup half-and-half

3¼ cups unsweetened almond milk

4 cups unsweetened cashew milk

¼ cup maple syrup

1 tablespoon vanilla extract

1 teaspoon allspice

Zest of 1 orange

Pinch of salt

Cashews, crushed, for garnish

Almonds, crushed, for garnish

Ful Medames

YIELD: 4 SERVINGS • ACTIVE TIME: 10 MINUTES
TOTAL TIME: 20 MINUTES

This beloved breakfast dish in Egypt is so enduring that it is said to have been enjoyed by the pharaohs.

INGREDIENTS

1 (14 oz.) can of fava beans, drained

4 garlic cloves, chopped

¼ cup olive oil, plus more to taste

Juice of 2 lemons

Salt and pepper, to taste

Large pinch of red pepper flakes

1 teaspoon cumin

2 hard-boiled eggs, each cut into 6 wedges

2 tablespoons minced parsley or mint, for garnish

Feta cheese, crumbled, for serving

Black olives, for serving

1 Place the beans and garlic in a Dutch oven, cover by ½" with water, and bring to a boil. Reduce the heat and simmer for 10 minutes.

2 Drain, transfer to a bowl, and add the olive oil, lemon juice, salt, pepper, red pepper flakes, and cumin. Lightly mash the beans with a fork and stir to combine.

3 Drizzle with additional olive oil, transfer to a platter, and place the pieces of hard-boiled egg on top. Garnish with parsley or mint and serve with the feta cheese and black olives.

INGREDIENTS
For the French Toast

8 eggs

2 tablespoons sugar

½ cup heavy cream

1 tablespoon cinnamon

1 tablespoon vanilla extract

Pinch of kosher salt

3 tablespoons unsalted butter

1 loaf of brioche, cut into 12 slices

For the Bananas Foster

1 stick unsalted butter

½ cup firmly packed light brown sugar

3 bananas, sliced

¼ cup dark rum

½ cup heavy cream

For Garnish

Confectioners' sugar

TIP: WHEN ADDING ALCOHOL TO HOT PANS, MAKE SURE YOU PULL THEM AWAY FROM HEAT BEFORE ADDING THE ALCOHOL. THIS WILL HELP YOU AVOID POTENTIAL FIRES AND INJURIES.

Bananas Foster French Toast

YIELD: 4 SERVINGS • ACTIVE TIME: 10 MINUTES
TOTAL TIME: 10 MINUTES

Incorporating elements of the classic New Orleans dessert makes this French toast as decadent as breakfast can get.

1 Preheat the oven to 200°F and place an oven-safe platter in it. To begin preparations for the French toast, place the eggs, sugar, heavy cream, cinnamon, vanilla, and salt in a mixing bowl and stir to combine.

2 Warm a 12" cast-iron skillet over medium-high heat and then add 1 tablespoon of the butter. When it has melted, dunk the slices of brioche in the batter to cover both sides. Working in batches, cook the brioche until a light brown crust forms on both sides, about 1 minute per side. Remove the cooked brioche slices from the pan and place them on the platter in the warm oven. Repeat until all of the brioche slices have been cooked, replenishing the butter in the skillet as needed.

3 To prepare the Bananas Foster, wipe out the skillet and add the stick of butter and the brown sugar. Once the butter and sugar have melted, add the bananas to the pan and cook for 3 minutes. Shake the pan and spoon the sauce over the bananas. Pull the pan away from the burner and add the rum. Using a long match or a lighter, carefully light the rum on fire. Place the pan back on the burner and shake the pan until the flames die out. Add the cream, stir to combine, and then pour the mixture over the French toast. Sprinkle the confectioners' sugar on top and serve.

PB & Banana Yogurt Bowl

**YIELD: 4 SERVINGS • ACTIVE TIME: 10 MINUTES
TOTAL TIME: 10 MINUTES**

Super quick, super delicious, and super nutritious. In other words, a super way to start the day.

INGREDIENTS

4 cups plain Greek yogurt

½ cup unsalted peanut butter

3 bananas

4 cups baby spinach

3 tablespoons chia seeds, plus ¼ cup for garnish

¼ cup unsweetened coconut flakes, for garnish

¼ cup peanuts, crushed, for garnish

1 Place all of the ingredients, except for the garnishes, in a food processor and puree until smooth.

2 Divide the mixture between the serving bowls, top each portion with the coconut, peanuts, and remaining chia seeds, and serve.

Soups & Salads

When pressed for time, we turn to the salad, tossing whatever's on hand into a bowl to provide our loved ones and ourselves with a shot of nutrition. When backed into a corner, we crave the comfort and sustenance that only a soup can provide. But they are not just for those times when the world has us against a wall. Often, soups and salads are the best ways to showcase a particular ingredient or incorporate an array of flavors, able to highlight elements that would get lost in other preparations.

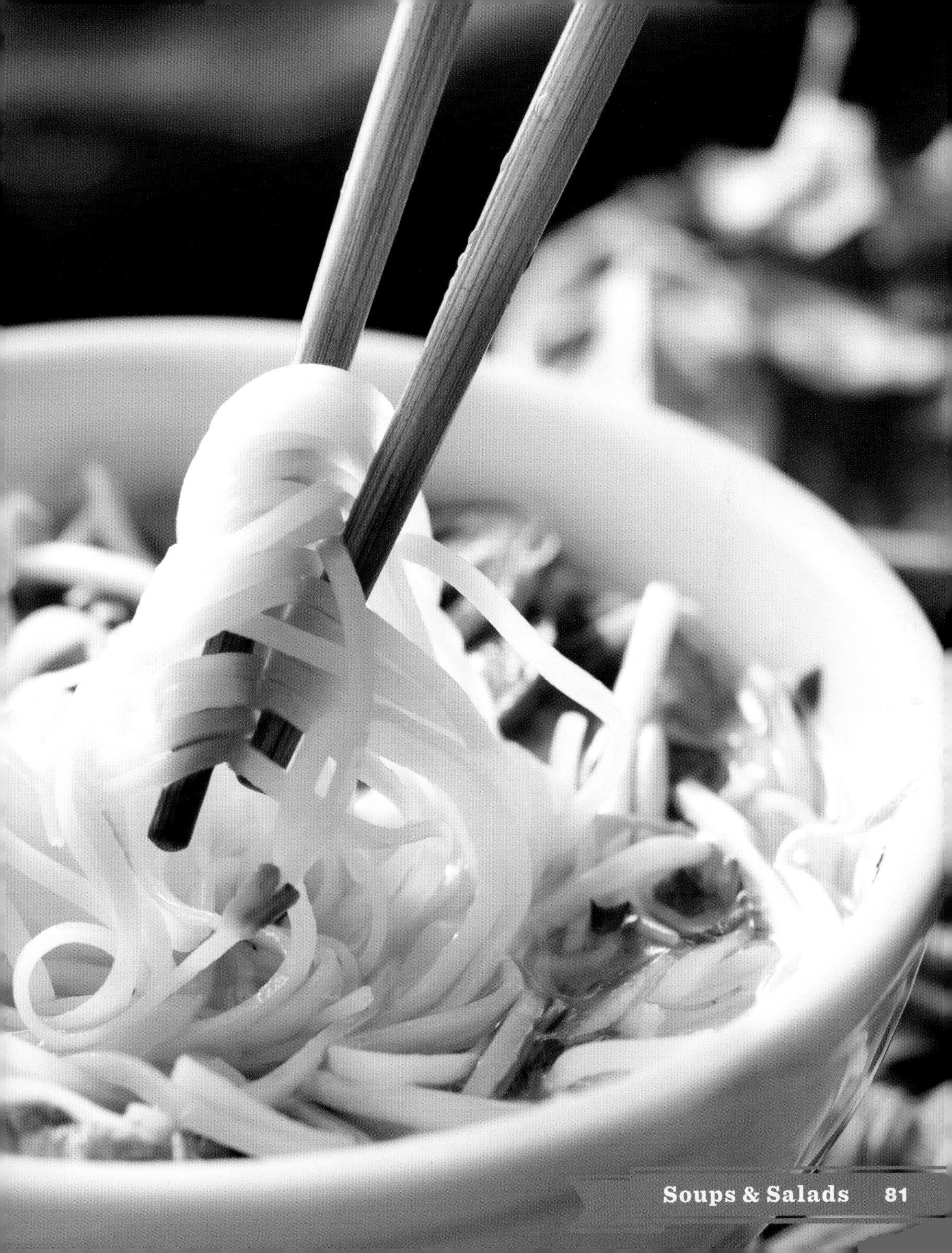

Spring Pea Soup

YIELD: 4 SERVINGS • ACTIVE TIME: 15 MINUTES
TOTAL TIME: 25 MINUTES

Early in the spring, peas are absolutely perfect—tender enough that they don't require a long cook time, and bursting with country fresh flavor.

1 Place the ricotta, cream, lemon zest, and 2 teaspoons of salt in a food processor and puree until smooth. Season to taste and set aside.

2 Place the water and remaining salt in a saucepan and bring to a boil over medium heat. Remove six long strips of zest from the lemon rind and add them to the saucepan with the peas and shallot. Cook for 2 to 3 minutes, until the peas are just cooked through. Drain, reserve 2 cups of the cooking liquid, and immediately transfer the peas, strips of lemon zest, and shallot to a blender. Add the mint leaves and half of the reserved cooking liquid and puree until the desired consistency is achieved, adding more of the reserved liquid as needed.

3 Season to taste, ladle into warmed bowls, and place a spoonful of the lemon ricotta in each bowl. Garnish with additional mint and

INGREDIENTS

1 cup ricotta cheese

¼ cup heavy cream

2 tablespoons lemon zest

2 teaspoons kosher salt plus 2 tablespoons

12 cups water

1 lemon rind

3 cups peas

3 small shallots, diced

6 mint leaves, plus more for garnish

Raspberry & Tomato Gazpacho

YIELD: 4 SERVINGS • ACTIVE TIME: 10 MINUTES
TOTAL TIME: 4 TO 24 HOURS

Countering the sweetness of roasted tomatoes with tart raspberries makes this chilled soup a hot commodity.

INGREDIENTS

2 to 3 large heirloom tomatoes

1 cup fresh raspberries

2 garlic cloves

½ cup peeled and sliced cucumber

2 teaspoons fresh lemon juice

2 tablespoons olive oil

1 red bell pepper, seeded and chopped

Salt and pepper, to taste

Mint leaves, for garnish

¼ cup heavy cream, for garnish (optional)

1 Preheat the oven to 425°F. Place the tomatoes on a baking sheet and bake until they start to break down and darken, about 10 to 15 minutes. Remove from the oven and let cool slightly.

2 Place the tomatoes and the remaining ingredients, except for the garnishes, in a blender and puree until smooth. Transfer the mixture to the refrigerator for at least 3 hours, though 24 hours in the refrigerator is recommended.

3 When ready to serve, ladle into bowls and garnish each serving with mint leaves and, if desired, approximately 1 tablespoon of heavy cream.

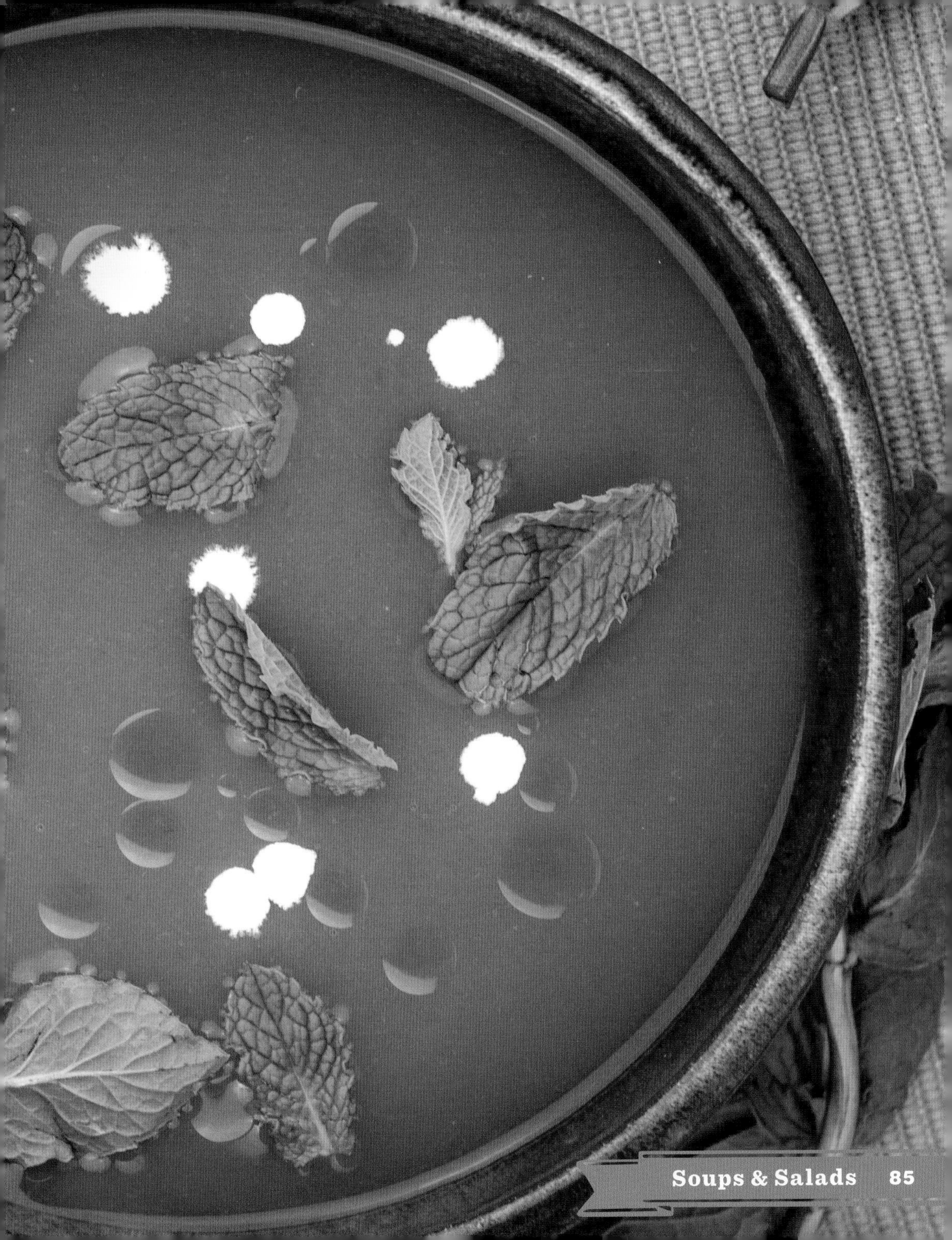

Zucchini Soup

The key to this little bit of heaven is browning the zucchini and onion so that the flavor really develops.

1 Place the butter in a Dutch oven and warm over medium heat until it starts to foam. Add the zucchini and onion and sauté until they start to brown, about 8 minutes. Add the garlic, oregano, dill seeds, and parsley and sauté until just fragrant, about 2 minutes. Reduce the heat, cover the Dutch oven, and let the vegetables sweat for 5 minutes.

2 Remove the lid and add the stock, white pepper, broccoli, and rice. Season with salt and bring to a simmer. Simmer for another 25 minutes.

3 Remove from heat and let it cool for a few minutes. Transfer to a blender and puree until smooth. Season to taste and garnish with the walnuts.

INGREDIENTS

2 tablespoons unsalted butter

2 large zucchini, chopped

1 large yellow onion, chopped

4 garlic cloves, minced

1 tablespoon dried oregano

1 tablespoon dill seeds

2 tablespoons dried parsley

6 cups Vegetable Stock
(see page 16)

1 teaspoon white pepper

2 cups broccoli florets

1 cup basmati rice

Salt, to taste

Walnuts, toasted and chopped,
for garnish

Dal

YIELD: 4 SERVINGS • ACTIVE TIME: 20 MINUTES
TOTAL TIME: 1½ HOURS

This simple stew of yellow peas, orange lentils, or mung beans is an everyday staple in most of India.

INGREDIENTS

2 tablespoons olive oil

1 yellow onion, diced

2 garlic cloves, minced

2 teaspoons red pepper flakes, or to taste

2 curry leaves (optional)

1 teaspoon kosher salt

1½ cups yellow split peas, picked over and rinsed

4 cups water

1 teaspoon turmeric

1 cup fresh peas

1 Place the olive oil in a Dutch oven and warm over medium-high heat. Add the onion, garlic, red pepper flakes, curry leaves (if using), and salt and sauté until the onion is slightly translucent, about 3 minutes.

2 Add the yellow split peas, water, and turmeric and bring to a simmer. Cover and gently simmer for 1 hour, stirring the dal two or three times as it simmers.

3 Remove the lid and simmer, while stirring occasionally, until the dal has thickened, about 30 minutes. When the dal has the consistency of porridge, stir in the peas, and cook until they are warmed through. Ladle the dal into warmed bowls and serve.

French Onion Soup

**YIELD: 6 SERVINGS • ACTIVE TIME: 1 HOUR
TOTAL TIME: 2½ HOURS**

This recipe is great if you've got a surplus of onions and some day-old bread you'd like to use up.

1 Place the butter, onions, and salt in a Dutch oven and cook over low heat while stirring often. Cook until the onions are dark brown and caramelized, about 40 minutes to 1 hour.

2 Deglaze the pot with the orange juice and Sherry. Use a wooden spoon to scrape any browned bits from the bottom. Add the thyme, stock, and garlic, raise the heat to medium, and bring to a simmer. Simmer for 1 hour.

3 While the soup is simmering, preheat the oven to 450°F. After 1 hour, ladle the soup into oven-safe bowls and place a slice of bread on top of each portion. Divide the cheeses between the bowls, place them in the oven, and bake until the cheese begins to brown, about 10 to 15 minutes. Carefully remove the bowls from the oven and let cool for 10 minutes before serving.

INGREDIENTS

3 tablespoons unsalted butter

7 large sweet onions, sliced

2 teaspoons kosher salt

⅓ cup orange juice

3 oz. Sherry

Leaves from 3 sprigs of thyme, minced

7 cups Beef Stock (see page 12)

3 garlic cloves, minced

2 teaspoons black pepper

6 slices of day-old bread

1 cup Gruyère cheese, shredded

1 cup Emmental cheese, shredded

Chili con Carne

Save this for a Sunday during football season: it's so good, it won't even matter if your team ends up losing.

1 Place the ground beef in a Dutch oven and cook, while breaking it up with a wooden spoon, over medium heat until it is browned.

2 Drain off the fat, add all of the remaining ingredients, except for the garnishes, and stir to combine. Bring to a boil, reduce the heat, and gently simmer, stirring occasionally, until the beans are fork-tender and the flavor is to your liking, 3 to 4 hours. Ladle into warmed bowls and garnish with the cheddar cheese, and the additional onions and cilantro.

Note: If you aren't a fan of spice, remove the seeds from the jalapeño, or just omit it entirely.

INGREDIENTS

1½ lbs. ground beef

1 (28 oz.) can of crushed San Marzano tomatoes

1 red bell pepper, stemmed, seeded, and diced

2 small yellow onions, diced, plus more for garnish

3 to 4 garlic cloves, minced

1 jalapeño pepper, stemmed and minced

1 lb. pink beans, soaked overnight and drained

¼ cup chopped fresh cilantro, plus more for garnish

¼ cup hot sauce

2 tablespoons chili powder

1 tablespoon black pepper

1 tablespoon kosher salt

2 tablespoons granulated garlic

⅓ cup cumin

1 tablespoon Madras curry powder

1 tablespoon dried oregano

Cheddar cheese, grated, for garnish

INGREDIENTS

1½ lbs. chuck steak, cut into 1" chunks

2 tablespoons kosher salt

1 tablespoon black pepper

1 tablespoon granulated onion

1 tablespoon granulated garlic

½ tablespoon dried oregano

1 teaspoon celery seeds

Pinch of red pepper flakes

2 tablespoons fresh thyme leaves, chopped

2 bay leaves

4 cups Beef Stock (see page 12)

3 garlic cloves, minced

3 carrots, peeled and diced

2 leeks, trimmed, rinsed well, and chopped

1 yellow onion, chopped

2 Yukon Gold potatoes, peeled and chopped

2 celery stalks, chopped

3 oz. tomato paste

2 tablespoons Worcestershire sauce

1 tablespoon soy sauce

¼ cup all-purpose flour

Beef Stew

YIELD: 4 SERVINGS • **ACTIVE TIME: 25 MINUTES**
TOTAL TIME: 6 TO 8 HOURS

This perfectly captures the beauty of the slow cooker: prepare it the night before, set on low before leaving in the morning, and come home to a house that smells amazing and a meal that's ready to go.

1 Place all of the ingredients, save the flour and 1 cup of the stock, in a slow cooker and stir to combine.

2 Place the flour and remaining stock in a bowl and stir until smooth. Add this mixture to the slow cooker and cover.

3 Cook on low until the beef and potatoes are extremely tender, 6 to 8 hours. Ladle into warmed bowls and serve.

Pho

**YIELD: 4 SERVINGS • ACTIVE TIME: 15 MINUTES
TOTAL TIME: 4 TO 8 HOURS**

This is a fairly traditional pho, but don't be afraid to be bold with your additions, as the possible variations are almost endless.

1 To prepare the broth, place all of the ingredients in a slow cooker, cover, and cook on low for at least 4 hours. For a very flavorful broth, cook for 8 hours.

2 Strain the broth through a fine sieve. Discard the solids and return the broth to the slow cooker. To begin preparations for the noodles and steak, add the noodles and bok choy to the broth, cover, and cook on low for approximately 30 minutes, until the noodles are tender and the bok choy is al dente.

3 Slice the steak into ⅛" thick pieces. Ladle the broth, noodles, and bok choy into bowls and top with the steak. The broth will cook the steak to rare. If you prefer the steak to be cooked more, add the slices to the slow cooker and cook in the broth for 2 to 3 minutes for medium-rare, 3 to 5 minutes for medium. Season with sriracha and ladle into warmed bowls.

Note: Popular toppings for pho include bean sprouts, sliced chili peppers, Thai basil, and scallions. Serve these alongside lime wedges and your own favorite toppings so everyone can tailor their bowl to taste.

INGREDIENTS
For the Broth

8 cups Beef Stock (see page 12)

1 large cinnamon stick

4 bay leaves

6 star anise pods

2 teaspoons kosher salt

2 teaspoons peppercorns

2 teaspoons coriander seeds

1 teaspoon allspice berries

1 teaspoon fennel seeds

¼ cup smashed fresh ginger

6 garlic cloves, smashed

4 lemongrass stalks, bruised

1 white onion, cut into 6 wedges

2 tablespoons dark soy sauce

2 tablespoons rice vinegar

2 tablespoons fish sauce

For the Noodles & Steak

½ lb. rice noodles

4 baby bok choy, washed and quartered

1½ lbs. N.Y. strip steak

Sriracha, to taste

Pozole

In Spanish, *pozole* means "hominy," a key ingredient in this traditional Mexican soup.

1 Drain the hominy and set it aside. Place the oil in a Dutch oven and warm over medium-high heat. When the oil starts to shimmer, add the pork and onion, season with salt and pepper, and cook, while stirring occasionally, until pork and onion are well browned, about 15 minutes.

2 Add the chipotles, hominy, thyme, and cumin. Cover with water and bring to a boil. Reduce heat and simmer, while stirring occasionally, until the pork and hominy are tender, about 1½ hours.

3 Stir in the garlic, cook for 5 minutes, and taste. Adjust seasoning if necessary, ladle the soup into warmed bowls, garnish with cilantro, and serve with lime wedges.

INGREDIENTS

2 cups dried hominy, soaked overnight

2 tablespoons olive oil

2 lbs. boneless pork shoulder, cut into 1" chunks

1 large yellow onion, chopped

Salt and pepper, to taste

4 dried chipotle peppers, halved, seeded, and chopped

2 tablespoons fresh thyme leaves, minced

2 tablespoons cumin

3 garlic cloves, minced

Cilantro, chopped, for garnish

Lime wedges, for serving

Chicken Noodle Soup

YIELD: 4 SERVINGS • ACTIVE TIME: 20 MINUTES
TOTAL TIME: 40 MINUTES

While the wide arms of the egg noodle are the most comforting, any type of noodle you have on hand will work here.

INGREDIENTS

1 tablespoon olive oil

2 (4 oz.) chicken breasts

½ yellow onion, minced

1 carrot, peeled and minced

1 celery stalk, minced

1 tablespoon fresh thyme leaves, minced

4 cups Chicken Stock (see page 11)

Salt and pepper, to taste

1½ cups egg noodles

1 Place the oil in a Dutch oven and warm over medium-high heat. When the oil starts to shimmer, add the chicken breasts and cook until they are browned on both sides and cooked through, about 5 minutes per side. Remove and set aside.

2 Add the onion and cook until it starts to soften, about 5 minutes. Add the carrot and celery, cook until tender, and then add the thyme and stock. Bring to a boil, reduce the heat, and simmer for 20 minutes. Chop the chicken into bite-sized pieces as the soup simmers.

3 Season the soup with salt and pepper, add the egg noodles and the chicken, and cook until the noodles are al dente, about 7 minutes. Ladle into warmed bowls and serve.

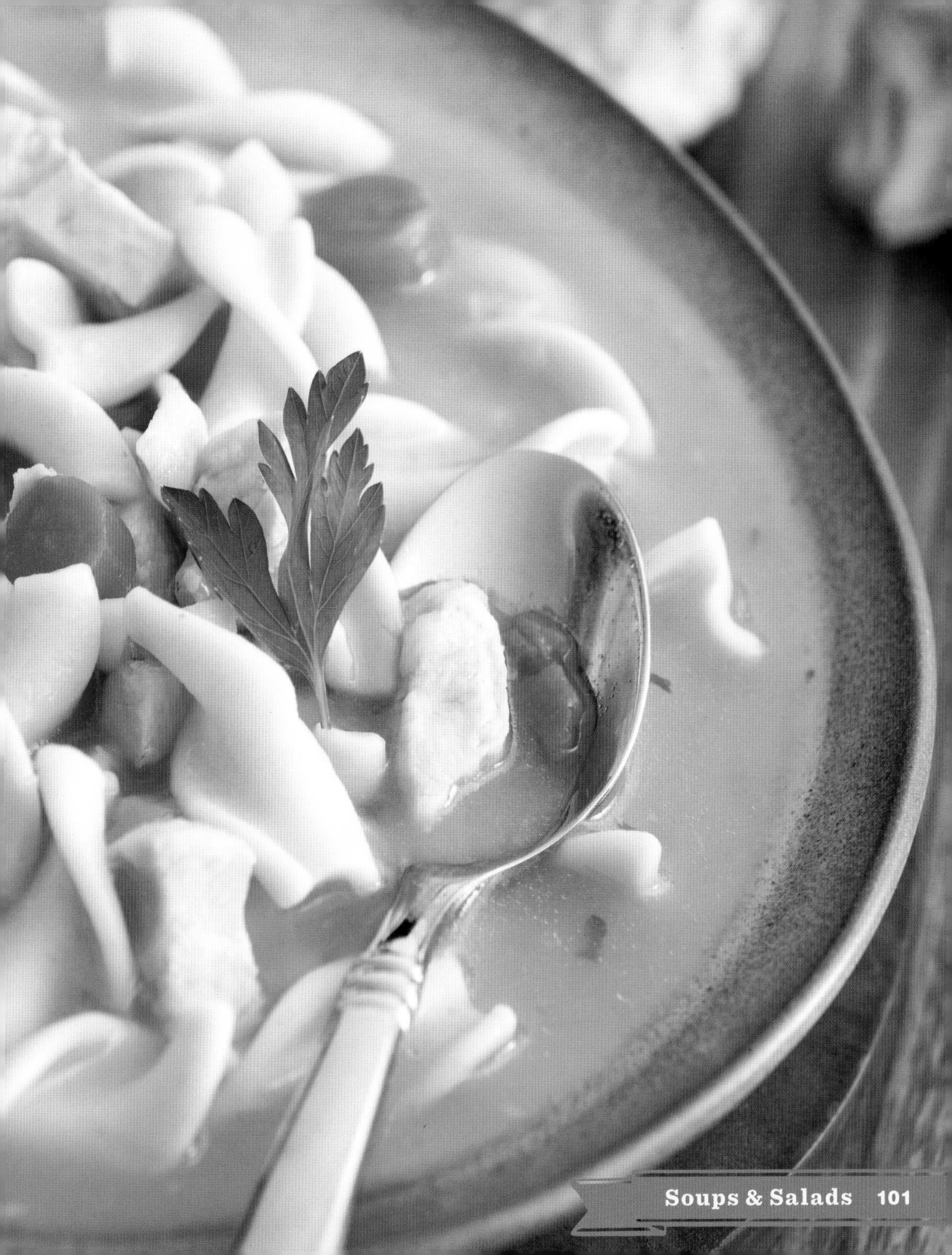

INGREDIENTS

½ lb. bacon, minced

2 tablespoons fresh thyme leaves, chopped

4 cups minced celery

4 Spanish onions, minced

4 tablespoons unsalted butter

6 garlic cloves, minced

⅓ cup all-purpose flour, plus 1 tablespoon

1½ lbs. creamer potatoes, minced

2 cups clam juice

2 tablespoons Worcestershire sauce

3 dashes of hot sauce

2 cups heavy cream

6 (6½ oz.) cans of cherrystone clams, with juice

Salt and pepper, to taste

Oyster crackers, for serving

Clam Chowder

**YIELD: 6 SERVINGS • ACTIVE TIME: 30 MINUTES
TOTAL TIME: 1½ HOURS**

Instead of spending a day sitting in traffic with the other leaf peepers, whip this up when you want a taste of fall in New England.

1 Place the bacon in a Dutch oven and cook, while stirring occasionally, over medium heat until it is crispy, about 8 minutes. Drain the fat from the pan and add the thyme, celery, onions, butter, and garlic. Reduce the heat to medium and cook until the onions are translucent, about 4 minutes. Add the ⅓ cup of flour and stir until all the vegetables are coated. Cook for 10 minutes, while frequently stirring and scraping the bottom of the pan to prevent anything from burning.

2 Add the potatoes and clam juice and cook until the potatoes are tender, about 20 minutes.

3 Add the Worcestershire sauce and hot sauce, stir, and then add the cream. Cook until the chowder is just thick enough to coat the back of a wooden spoon. Add the clams and cook until they are heated through, about 10 minutes. Season with salt and pepper, ladle into warmed bowls, and serve with oyster crackers.

Crab & Okra Soup

YIELD: 4 SERVINGS • ACTIVE TIME: 10 MINUTES
TOTAL TIME: 25 MINUTES

If you're not already familiar, the combination of peanuts, coconut, and clam juice will be a revelation.

1 Place the peanuts in a large, dry Dutch oven and toast over medium heat until they are browned. Remove them from the pan and set aside. Add the okra and cook, while stirring, until browned all over, about for 5 minutes. Remove and set aside.

2 Place the coconut oil in the Dutch oven and warm over medium heat. When it starts to shimmer, add the bell pepper, onion, habanero pepper, and potato and sauté until the onion starts to soften, about 5 minutes.

3 Add the stock and clam juice, bring to a simmer, and cook for 5 minutes. Add the coconut milk, return to a simmer, and season with salt.

4 Working in batches, transfer the soup to a blender and puree until smooth. Return the soup to the Dutch oven and simmer for another 5 minutes. Stir in the peanuts, okra, spinach, and crabmeat and cook until the spinach has wilted. Ladle the soup into warmed bowls and serve with lime wedges.

INGREDIENTS

1 cup peanuts, chopped

10 okra pods, sliced into ½" rounds

½ cup coconut oil

1 red bell pepper, stemmed, seeded, and diced

1 yellow onion, sliced into half-moons

1 habanero pepper, stemmed, seeded, and chopped

1 large potato, peeled and diced

4 cups Vegetable Stock (see page 16)

1 cup clam juice

1 cup coconut milk

Salt, to taste

4 cups baby spinach

1 lb. lump crabmeat

Lime wedges, for serving

INGREDIENTS
For the Salad

1 tablespoon kosher salt, plus 2 teaspoons

½ lb. pearl onions, trimmed

Kernels from 1 ear of corn

1 cup chopped green beans

4 cups day-old bread pieces

2 cups chopped overripe tomatoes

10 large basil leaves, torn

Black pepper, to taste

For the Vinaigrette

½ cup white balsamic vinegar

¼ cup olive oil

2 tablespoons minced shallot

¼ cup sliced scallions

2 tablespoons chopped parsley leaves

2 teaspoons kosher salt

1 teaspoon black pepper

Panzanella with White Balsamic Vinaigrette

YIELD: 4 SERVINGS • ACTIVE TIME: 25 MINUTES
TOTAL TIME: 45 MINUTES

When caught in the breakneck pace of the summer, quick dishes that can salvage ingredients that have lingered slightly too long are extremely valuable. This salad is one such treasure.

1 To begin preparations for the salad, bring water to boil in a small saucepan and prepare an ice water bath in a mixing bowl. When the water is boiling, add the 1 tablespoon of salt and the pearl onions and cook for 5 minutes. When the onions have 1 minute left to cook, add the corn and green beans to the saucepan and cook for 1 minute. Transfer the vegetables to the ice water bath and let cool completely.

2 Remove the pearl onions from the water bath and squeeze to remove the bulbs from their skins. Cut the bulbs in half and break them down into individual petals. Drain the corn and green beans and pat dry. Set the vegetables aside.

3 To prepare the vinaigrette, place all of the ingredients in a mixing bowl and whisk until combined.

4 Place the blanched vegetables, bread, tomatoes, and basil in a salad bowl and toss to combine. Add the remaining salt, season with pepper, and add half of the vinaigrette. Toss to evenly coat, taste, and add more of the vinaigrette if desired.

Chilled Corn Salad

This recipe is a riff on a classic Mexican dish known as *esquites*, and it can easily be altered to suit your family's taste and the changing seasons.

1 Preheat the oven to 400°F. Place the corn on a baking sheet, place it in the oven, and bake until it turns a light golden brown, about 35 minutes.

2 Remove the corn from the oven, let it cool slightly, and then transfer to a large mixing bowl. Add the remaining ingredients and stir to combine.

3 Place the salad in the refrigerator and chill for at least 3 hours, although letting it chill overnight is highly recommended.

INGREDIENTS

2 cups corn kernels

2 tablespoons unsalted butter

1 jalapeño pepper, stemmed, seeded, and diced

2 tablespoons mayonnaise

2 teaspoons garlic powder

3 tablespoons sour cream

¼ teaspoon cayenne pepper

¼ teaspoon chili powder

2 tablespoons feta cheese

2 tablespoons Cotija cheese

2 teaspoons fresh lime juice

½ cup chopped fresh cilantro

Salt and pepper, to taste

4 cups lettuce or arugula

Sofrito & Quinoa Salad

YIELD: 4 SERVINGS • ACTIVE TIME: 15 MINUTES
TOTAL TIME: 4 HOURS

This twist on traditional Spanish rice gives you the flavor you crave while adding protein in the form of quinoa and pumpkin seeds.

1 Dice one of the poblanos, half of the bell peppers, and half of the onion. Place these to the side. Add the remaining ingredients, except for the quinoa and the pumpkin seeds, to a blender or food processor and puree until smooth.

2 Place the diced vegetables, the puree, and the quinoa in a slow cooker and cook on low until the quinoa is fluffy, about 4 hours.

3 Garnish with the pumpkin seeds and serve.

INGREDIENTS

2 poblano peppers, stemmed and seeded

1 red bell pepper, stemmed and seeded

1 green bell pepper, stemmed and seeded

1 white onion, peeled and cut into quarters

3 plum tomatoes

2 garlic cloves

1 tablespoon cumin

2 tablespoons adobo seasoning

1½ cups quinoa, rinsed

Toasted pumpkin seeds, for garnish

Cauliflower & Chickpea Salad

YIELD: 4 SERVINGS • ACTIVE TIME: 25 MINUTES
TOTAL TIME: 45 MINUTES

Crunchy cauliflower, nutty chickpeas, and a perfect balance of sweet and spicy makes this salad a showstopper.

1 Preheat the oven to 400°F.

2 To prepare the salad, place all of the ingredients in a mixing bowl and toss to coat. Place the mixture in a 9 x 13-inch baking pan, place the pan in the oven, and bake until the cauliflower is slightly charred and still crunchy, about 30 minutes. Remove from the oven and let the mixture cool slightly.

3 To prepare the dressing, place all of the ingredients in the mixing bowl and stir until the sugar is dissolved. Place the cooked cauliflower-and-chickpea mixture in the bowl, toss to coat, and serve.

INGREDIENTS
For the Salad

1 (14 oz.) can of chickpeas, drained

3 cups chopped cauliflower florets

3 garlic cloves, sliced thin

1 shallot, sliced thin

⅓ cup olive oil

½ teaspoon dark chili powder

½ teaspoon chipotle powder

½ teaspoon black pepper

½ teaspoon onion powder

½ teaspoon garlic powder

¼ teaspoon paprika

1 tablespoon kosher salt

For the Dressing

2 scallions, sliced thin

2 Fresno peppers, stemmed, seeded, and sliced thin

3 tablespoons sugar

¼ cup red wine vinegar

½ teaspoon dark chili powder

½ teaspoon chipotle powder

½ teaspoon black pepper

½ teaspoon onion powder

½ teaspoon garlic powder

¼ teaspoon paprika

½ tablespoon kosher salt

INGREDIENTS
For the Peanut Sauce

Juice of 2 limes

2 tablespoons minced ginger

1 garlic clove

¼ cup brown sugar

2 tablespoons fish sauce

2 tablespoons soy sauce

½ cup peanut butter

For the Salad

1 lb. rice stick noodles

½ lb. carrots, peeled and sliced thin

1 red bell pepper, stemmed, seeded, and sliced thin

1 Fresno pepper, stemmed, seeded, and sliced thin

2 jalapeño peppers, stemmed, seeded, and julienned

4 scallions, sliced thin on a bias

1 cup fresh basil

¼ cup chopped fresh cilantro

2 tablespoons chopped fresh mint

Peanuts, crushed, for garnish

Rice Noodle Salad

Perfect for those hot summer nights when you're terrified by the prospect of turning on the oven.

1 To prepare the peanut sauce, place all of the ingredients in a blender and puree until smooth. Transfer to the refrigerator and chill overnight.

2 To begin preparations for the salad, bring water to a boil in a large saucepan and add the noodles. Cook, while stirring, until the noodles are just tender, about 3 minutes. Drain and rinse with cold water.

3 Place the noodles and the remaining ingredients, except for the peanuts, in a salad bowl. Stir to combine, add the peanut sauce, and toss to coat. Garnish with the crushed peanuts and serve.

Melon & Prosciutto Salad

YIELD: 4 SERVINGS • ACTIVE TIME: 15 MINUTES
TOTAL TIME: 45 MINUTES

As this dynamic salad shows, the versatile melon can comfortably sit on either side of the sweet-and-savory divide.

1 Preheat the oven to 350°F. To begin preparations for the salad, place the prosciutto on a parchment–lined baking sheet. Place in the oven and bake until the prosciutto is crisp, about 8 minutes. Remove from the oven and let cool. When the prosciutto is cool enough to handle, chop it into bite-sized pieces.

2 To prepare the vinaigrette, place all of the ingredients in a mixing bowl and whisk until thoroughly combined. Set aside.

3 Place the cantaloupe, honeydew melon, and cucumber in a salad bowl, season with salt and pepper, and toss to combine. Add the jalapeño and vinaigrette and toss until evenly coated. Plate the salad, top with the chopped prosciutto and feta, and garnish with mint leaves.

INGREDIENTS

For the Salad

8 slices of prosciutto

3 cups diced cantaloupe

3 cups diced honeydew melon

2 cups sliced cucumber

Salt and pepper, to taste

1 jalapeño pepper, stemmed, seeded, and sliced

$^2/_3$ cup feta cheese

Mint leaves, chopped, for garnish

For the Vinaigrette

3 tablespoons chopped fresh mint

¼ cup olive oil

3 tablespoons apple cider vinegar

1 tablespoon honey

2 teaspoons diced shallot

1 teaspoon kosher salt

¼ teaspoon black pepper

INGREDIENTS

1½ lbs. boneless, skinless chicken breasts, halved along the equator

Salt and pepper, to taste

Dash of olive oil

1 cup mayonnaise

3 tablespoons fresh lime juice

¼ cup Madras curry powder

1 tablespoon cumin

1 tablespoon granulated garlic

½ teaspoon cinnamon

½ teaspoon turmeric

2 cups minced celery

2 Granny Smith apples, minced

½ red bell pepper, stemmed, seeded, and minced

¾ cup pecans, chopped

5 to 6 oz. baby arugula

Curried Chicken Salad

YIELD: 6 SERVINGS • ACTIVE TIME: 15 MINUTES
TOTAL TIME: 45 MINUTES

If you'd prefer to make sandwiches with this salad, toasted marble rye is the best bread option by far.

1 Preheat the oven to 350°F. Place the chicken on a baking sheet, season with salt and pepper, and drizzle with olive oil. Place the chicken in the oven and bake until the center of each breast reaches 160°F, about 30 minutes. Remove the chicken from the oven and let rest for 10 minutes.

2 Place the mayonnaise, lime juice, and all of the seasonings in a salad bowl and stir to combine. Add the celery, apples, bell pepper, and ½ cup of the pecans and stir to incorporate.

3 Once the chicken has cooled, dice the breasts into small cubes and add to the salad bowl. Add the arugula, toss to combine, and serve.

Couscous & Shrimp Salad

**YIELD: 6 SERVINGS • ACTIVE TIME: 40 MINUTES
TOTAL TIME: 50 MINUTES**

Don't hesitate to go for seconds of this salad, which is light and packed with protein.

1 Place the shrimp, mint, and garlic in a Dutch oven and cover with water. Bring to a simmer over medium heat and cook until the shrimp are pink and cooked through, about 5 minutes after the water comes to a simmer. Drain, cut the shrimp in half lengthwise, and them set aside. Discard the mint and garlic cloves.

2 Place the stock in the Dutch oven and bring to a boil. Add the couscous, reduce the heat so that the stock simmers, cover, and cook until the couscous is tender and has absorbed the stock, 7 to 10 minutes. Transfer the couscous to a salad bowl.

3 Fill the pot with water and bring to a boil. Add the asparagus and cook until it has softened, 1 to 1½ minutes. Drain, rinse under cold water, and chop into bite-sized pieces. Pat the asparagus dry.

4 Add all of the remaining ingredients, except for the feta, to the salad bowl containing the couscous. Add the asparagus and stir to incorporate. Top with the shrimp and the feta and serve.

INGREDIENTS

¾ lb. shrimp, shelled and deveined

6 bunches of mint

10 garlic cloves

3½ cups Chicken Stock (see page 11)

3 cups Israeli couscous

1 bunch of asparagus, woody ends removed

3 plum tomatoes, diced

1 tablespoon chopped fresh oregano

½ English cucumber, diced

Zest and juice of 1 lemon

½ cup diced red onion

½ cup thinly sliced sun-dried tomatoes

¼ cup pitted and chopped Kalamata olives

⅓ cup olive oil

Salt and pepper, to taste

½ cup crumbled feta cheese

Beef, Pork & Lamb

If you flipped directly to this chapter, we understand. The ease, affordability, and flavor available in the members of this trio attract almost everyone when it's time to hatch a plan for dinner. But along with this inclination comes the potential to overindulge in specific preparations, robbing these meats of the magic that makes them so appealing in the first place. With that in mind, we take you on a whirlwind tour of world cuisines, introducing dishes like Rogan Josh (see pages 154–155) or Crying Tiger Beef (see pages 128–129) to keep your work in the kitchen from getting stale.

Carne Asada

YIELD: 4 SERVINGS • ACTIVE TIME: 30 MINUTES
TOTAL TIME: 3 HOURS

Most people make this on the grill, but even fire cannot equal the power of a cast-iron skillet here.

1 Place all of the ingredients, except for the steak and the tortillas, in a large resealable plastic bag and stir to combine. Add the steak, place it in the refrigerator, and let marinate for at least 2 hours. If time allows, marinate the steak overnight.

2 Approximately 30 minutes before you are going to cook the steak, remove it from the marinade, pat it dry, and let it come to room temperature.

3 Place a 12" cast-iron skillet over high heat and add enough oil to coat the bottom. When the oil starts to shimmer, add the steak and cook on each side for 6 minutes for medium-rare.

4 Remove the steak from the pan and let rest for 5 minutes before slicing it into thin strips, making sure to cut against the grain. Serve with the tortillas and your favorite taco toppings.

INGREDIENTS

1 jalapeño pepper, seeded and minced

3 garlic cloves, minced

½ cup chopped fresh cilantro

¼ cup olive oil, plus more as needed

Juice of 1 small orange

2 tablespoons apple cider vinegar

2 teaspoons cayenne pepper

1 teaspoon ancho chili powder

1 teaspoon garlic powder

1 teaspoon paprika

1 teaspoon kosher salt

1 teaspoon cumin

1 teaspoon dried oregano

¼ teaspoon black pepper

2 lbs. flank or skirt steak, trimmed

Corn tortillas (see page 23 for homemade), for serving

INGREDIENTS

½ cup olive oil

2 garlic cloves, minced

2 teaspoons
Worcestershire sauce

2 teaspoons red wine vinegar

1 tablespoon mustard powder

2 lbs. sirloin, sliced thin

2 yellow onions, chopped

2 red bell peppers, stemmed,
seeded, and chopped

Salt and pepper, to taste

Steak with Peppers & Onions

**YIELD: 4 SERVINGS • ACTIVE TIME: 20 MINUTES
TOTAL TIME: 3 HOURS**

If you somehow end up with leftovers, put them on a crusty French roll with some arugula.

1 Place 7 tablespoons of the oil in a large bowl. Add the garlic, Worcestershire sauce, red wine vinegar, and mustard powder and stir to combine. Add the sirloin and stir until coated. Cover and refrigerate for 2 hours, while stirring once or twice. If time allows, let the sirloin marinate overnight.

2 Approximately 30 minutes before you are ready to cook, remove the sirloin from the marinade and allow to come to room temperature.

3 Place a 12" cast-iron skillet over medium-high heat and coat the bottom with the remaining oil. When it starts to shimmer, add the sirloin and cook until browned all over, about 8 minutes. Remove from the pan and set aside.

4 Reduce the heat to medium, add the onions and peppers, and cook, without stirring, until they are browned, about 5 minutes. Return the sirloin to the pan and cook for an additional 2 minutes. Season with salt and pepper and serve immediately.

Crying Tiger Beef

YIELD: 4 SERVINGS • ACTIVE TIME: 15 MINUTES
TOTAL TIME: 30 MINUTES

Don't be thrown by the name—the only tears resulting from this dish are those of joy.

INGREDIENTS

2 lbs. flank steak

2 tablespoons soy sauce

1 tablespoon oyster sauce

1 tablespoon brown sugar, plus 1 teaspoon

1 large tomato, diced and seeded

⅓ cup fresh lime juice

¼ cup fish sauce (optional)

2 tablespoons minced fresh cilantro

1½ tablespoons Toasted Rice Powder (see sidebar)

1 tablespoon red pepper flakes

1 cup soft herb leaf mix (mint, basil, and cilantro), for garnish

1 Pat the steak dry. Place it in a bowl and add the soy sauce, oyster sauce, and tablespoon of brown sugar. Stir to combine and then let the steak marinate for 10 minutes.

2 Place a cast-iron skillet over high heat and spray it with nonstick cooking spray. Add the steak and cook on each side for 5 minutes for medium. Transfer to a plate, cover with foil, and let rest for 5 minutes before slicing into thin strips, making sure to cut against the grain.

3 Place the tomato, lime juice, fish sauce (if using), remaining brown sugar, cilantro, Toasted Rice Powder, and red pepper flakes in a bowl and stir to combine. The powder won't dissolve, but it will lightly bind the rest of the ingredients together. Divide the sauce between the serving bowls. Top with the slices of beef and garnish each portion with the soft herb leaf mix.

Toasted Rice Powder

INGREDIENTS

½ **cup jasmine rice**

1 Warm a cast-iron skillet over medium-high heat. Add the rice and toast until it starts to brown.

2 Remove and grind into a fine powder with a mortar and pestle.

TIP: IF YOU'RE ABLE TO TRACK IT DOWN, THAI HOLY BASIL WILL TAKE THIS DISH UP ANOTHER LEVEL.

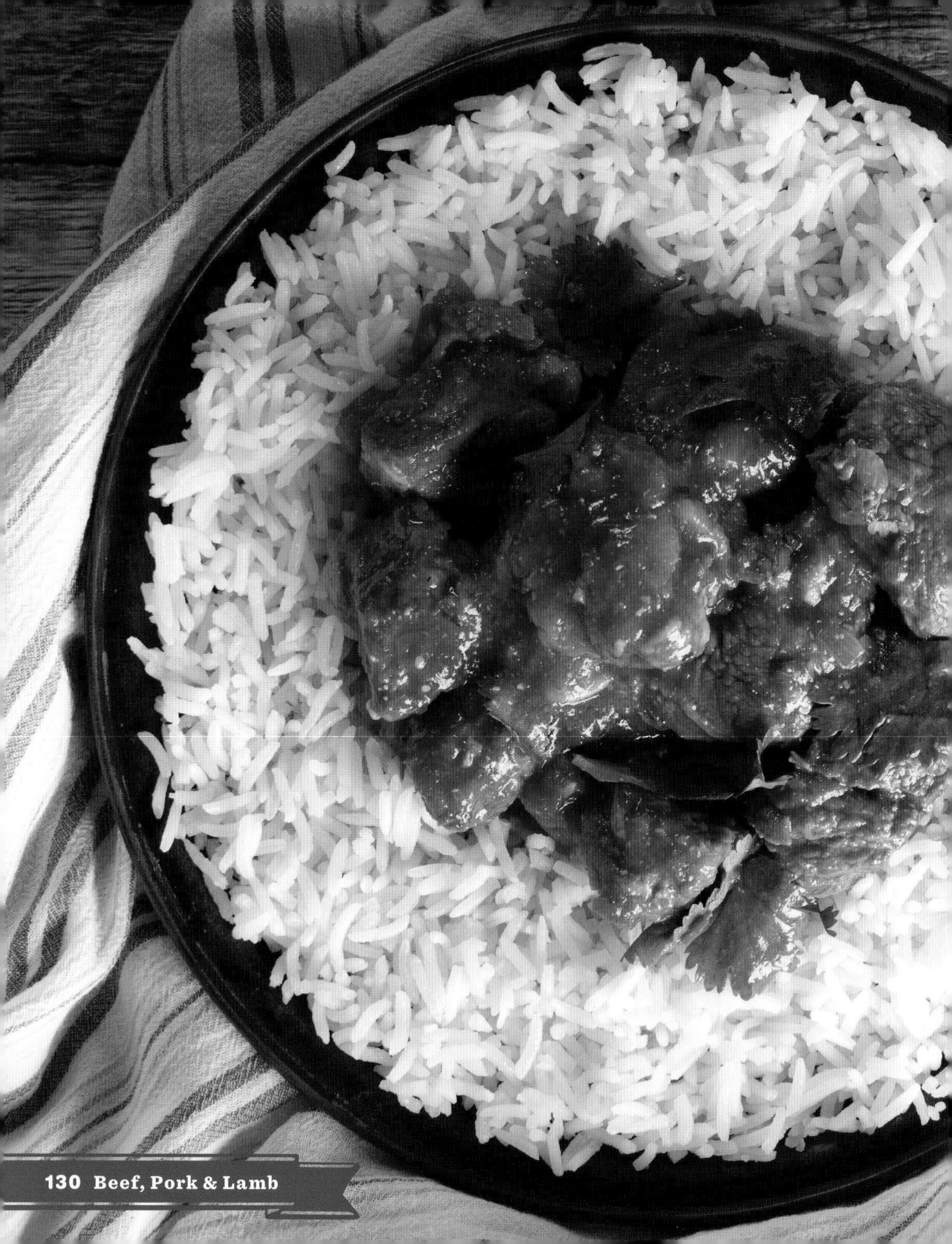

Sichuan Cumin Beef

YIELD: 4 SERVINGS • ACTIVE TIME: 10 MINUTES
TOTAL TIME: 2 HOURS AND 15 MINUTES

This extremely fragrant recipe possesses equally heady flavors thanks to the unique buzz the Sichuan peppercorn supplies.

1 Place the cumin seeds and Sichuan peppercorns in a dry 12" cast-iron skillet and toast over medium heat until they are fragrant, about 1 minute. Do not let them burn. Remove and grind to a fine powder with a mortar and pestle.

2 Place the salt, 2 tablespoons of the oil, the dried chilies, red pepper flakes, and the toasted spice powder into a large bowl and stir to combine. Add the chuck steak and toss until coated. Cover the bowl and let stand for 2 hours.

3 Warm the cast-iron skillet over high heat until the pan is extremely hot, about 10 minutes. Add the remaining oil, swirl to coat, and then add the steak and onion. Cook, while stirring occasionally, until the beef is browned all over, about 10 minutes. Garnish with the scallions and cilantro and serve immediately.

INGREDIENTS

3 tablespoons cumin seeds

2 teaspoons
Sichuan peppercorns

1 teaspoon kosher salt

3 tablespoons olive oil

4 dried red chili peppers

2 teaspoons red pepper flakes

1½ lbs. chuck steak, cut
into 1" pieces

1 yellow onion, sliced

2 scallions, sliced thin,
for garnish

½ cup chopped fresh cilantro,
for garnish

Sukiyaki

**YIELD: 4 SERVINGS • ACTIVE TIME: 5 MINUTES
TOTAL TIME: 15 MINUTES**

This modest Japanese preparation will quickly become a family favorite.

INGREDIENTS

Salt, to taste

1½ lbs. udon noodles

1 tablespoon olive oil

3 tablespoons brown sugar

2 lbs. rib eye, sliced very thin

½ cup mirin

½ cup sake

⅓ cup soy sauce

1 cup Dashi Broth (see page 19) or water

1 bunch of scallions, sliced into 2" pieces

2 cups chopped Napa cabbage

1 bunch of enoki mushrooms

6 large shiitake mushrooms

1 cup fresh spinach

½ lb. tofu, drained and cut into ¼" cubes

1 Bring salted water to a boil in a Dutch oven. Add the noodles to the boiling water and cook for 2 minutes. Drain, rinse with cold water, and set the noodles aside.

2 Place the olive oil in the Dutch oven and warm over medium-high heat. When the oil starts to shimmer, add the brown sugar and steak and cook until the steak is browned all over, about 2 minutes. Add the mirin, sake, soy sauce, and Dashi Broth or water and stir to combine.

3 Carefully arrange the noodles, scallions, cabbage, mushrooms, spinach, and tofu in the broth. Cover and steam until the cabbage is wilted. Ladle into warmed bowls and serve immediately.

Dry Rub

INGREDIENTS

¼ cup ground coffee

1 teaspoon ground coriander

2 teaspoons black pepper

Pinch of red pepper flakes

1 teaspoon cumin

2 teaspoons mustard powder

2 teaspoons dark chili powder

1 teaspoon paprika

6 tablespoons kosher salt

6 tablespoons light brown sugar

1 Place all of the ingredients in a mixing bowl and stir to combine. Transfer the mixture to an airtight container and store for up to 6 months.

Coffee & Bourbon Brisket

YIELD: 6 SERVINGS • ACTIVE TIME: 15 MINUTES
TOTAL TIME: 8½ HOURS

You'll learn to love this marriage of Texan and Southern BBQ, where the slight bitterness of coffee and sweet bourbon work beautifully together.

1 To prepare the brisket, place the onion, peach, nectarine, and ginger in a slow cooker. Apply the Dry Rub to the brisket and place the brisket on top of the mixture in the slow cooker. Add the water, cover, and cook on low for 6 hours.

2 Remove the contents of the slow cooker, transfer the brisket to a mixing bowl or cutting board, and discard everything else. Place all of the ingredients for the BBQ sauce in the slow cooker and cook on high for 1 hour.

3 Return the brisket to the slow cooker, reduce the heat to low, and cook for another hour. Remove the brisket from the slow cooker, let rest for 30 minutes, and then use a sharp knife to cut it into ½" slices against the grain.

INGREDIENTS
For the Brisket

1 yellow onion, diced

1 peach, pitted and minced

1 nectarine, pitted and minced

1 tablespoon minced ginger

½ cup Dry Rub (see sidebar)

3½ lbs. flat-cut brisket

1 cup water

For the Coffee & Bourbon BBQ Sauce

2 cups brewed coffee

¼ cup dark brown sugar

¾ cup bourbon

3 tablespoons molasses

¼ cup raw apple cider vinegar

2 tablespoons Worcestershire sauce

¼ cup ketchup

1 tablespoon granulated garlic

½ tablespoon black pepper, coarsely ground

1 tablespoon tapioca starch or cornstarch

Yankee Short Ribs

**YIELD: 4 SERVINGS • ACTIVE TIME: 30 MINUTES
TOTAL TIME: 3½ HOURS**

A wonderful twist on a New England classic—the Yankee pot roast.

1 Preheat the oven to 300°F. Place the oil in a Dutch oven and warm it over medium-high heat. Pat the short ribs dry and season generously with salt. Working in batches, place the short ribs in the Dutch oven and cook, while turning, until they are browned all over. Transfer the cooked short ribs to a paper towel–lined plate.

2 Place all of the short ribs in the pot, add the onions, carrots, potatoes, stock, and bay leaves to the Dutch oven, cover, and place it in the oven. Cook until the short ribs are fork-tender and the meat easily comes away from the bone, 3 to 4 hours.

3 Remove the pot from the oven, strain the contents through a fine sieve, making sure to reserve the cooking liquid, discard the bay leaves, and place the short ribs and vegetables in a mixing bowl. Place the reserved liquid in a pan with the rosemary, thyme, and red wine. Cook over high heat until the mixture has reduced and started to thicken.

4 Season the sauce with salt and pepper. Divide the short ribs and vegetables between the serving plates and spoon 2 to 3 tablespoons of the sauce over each portion.

INGREDIENTS

2 tablespoons olive oil

4 lbs. bone-in beef short ribs

Salt and pepper, to taste

2 large onions, sliced

4 carrots, peeled and diced

4 large potatoes, peeled and diced

8 cups Beef Stock (see page 12)

4 bay leaves

2 sprigs of rosemary

2 sprigs of thyme

½ cup red wine

Skillet Meatloaf with Bacon

YIELD: 6 SERVINGS • ACTIVE TIME: 10 MINUTES
TOTAL TIME: 1 HOUR

This dish is a standard in most American homes because it's good enough to eat every single day.

1 Preheat the oven to 375°F. Place the beef, pork, onion, garlic powder, bread crumbs, milk, eggs, tomato paste, and Worcestershire sauce in a bowl and use a wooden spoon or your hands to combine.

2 Coat the bottom of a 10" cast-iron skillet with the olive oil. Place the meat mixture in the pan and form it into a dome. Place five slices of bacon over the top and place the other five on top in the opposite direction, weaving them together.

3 Place the skillet in the oven and bake for 45 minutes. Remove and let cool for 10 minutes before slicing the meatloaf.

INGREDIENTS

1½ lbs. ground beef

½ lb. ground pork

1 yellow onion, minced

2 teaspoons garlic powder

1 cup bread crumbs

¼ cup whole milk

2 eggs, lightly beaten

2 tablespoons tomato paste

2 tablespoons
Worcestershire sauce

2 teaspoons olive oil

10 slices of bacon

Beef & Pork Burgers

YIELD: 6 SERVINGS • ACTIVE TIME: 10 MINUTES
TOTAL TIME: 25 MINUTES

The secret to a perfect burger is using a mixture of beef and pork, as this guarantees the juicy result everyone craves.

INGREDIENTS

1 lb. ground beef

1 lb. ground pork

Salt and pepper, to taste

6 brioche buns, toasted

6 slices of pepper jack cheese

1 Place the beef and pork in a mixing bowl, season with salt and pepper, and stir to combine.

2 Place a cast-iron skillet over medium-high heat. Form the beef-and-pork mixture into six evenly sized balls and then press down until they are patties. When the skillet is hot, place the burgers in the skillet and cook for 8 to 10 minutes. Flip the burgers over and cook until completely cooked through, about 5 to 8 minutes. Since the burgers contain pork, it is important to cook them all the way through. If you're worried that they will dry out, don't fret. The pork fat will keep the burgers moist and flavorful.

3 Assemble the cooked burgers using the brioche buns and cheese.

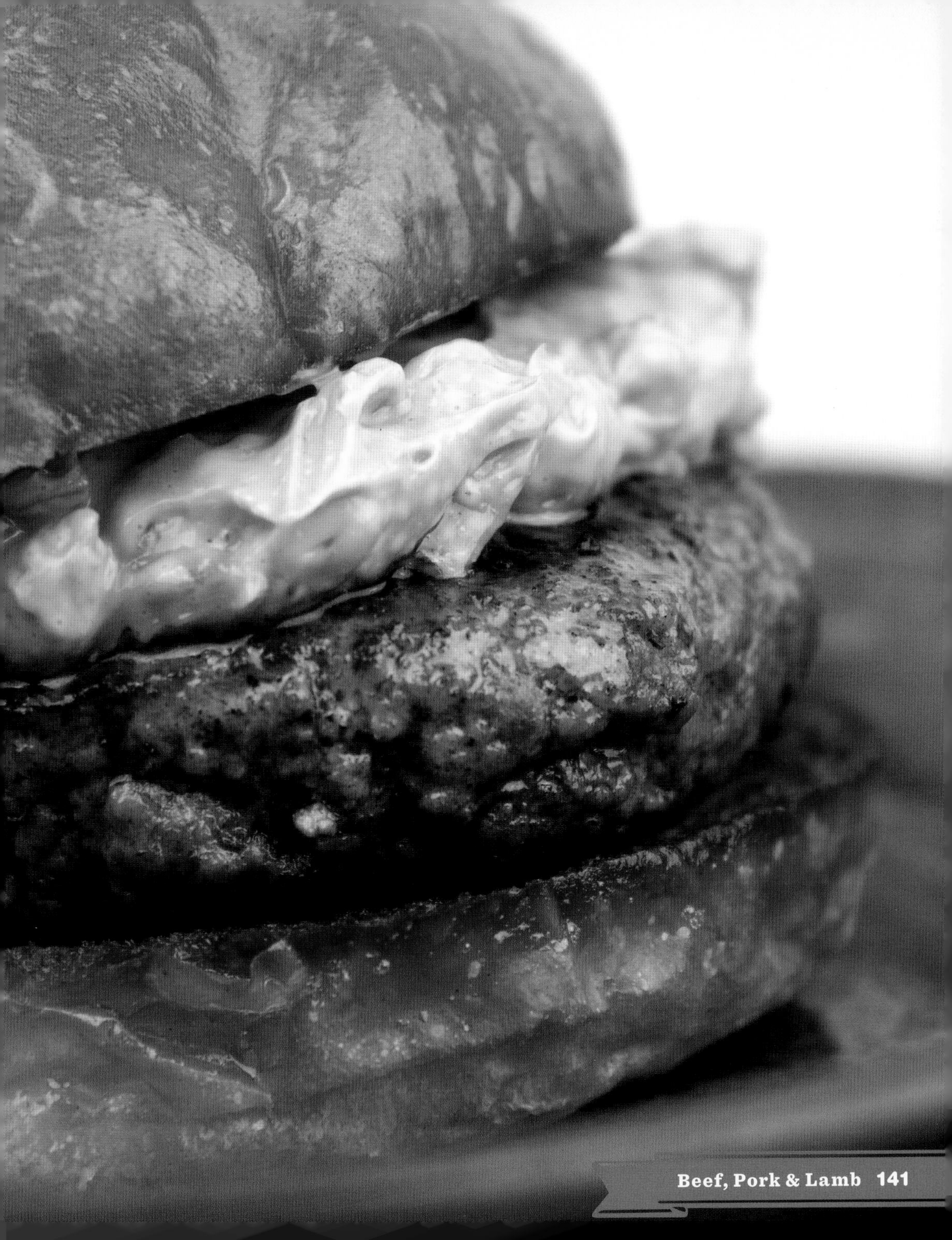

5- to 6-lb., skin-on pork belly

1 tablespoon fresh rosemary leaves, minced

1 tablespoon fresh thyme leaves, minced

1 tablespoon minced fresh sage leaves

2 teaspoons garlic powder

Salt, to taste

1-lb. center-cut pork tenderloin

Porchetta

If you've never had this crispy, tender, rich wonder, be prepared to fall madly in love.

1 Place the pork belly skin-side down on a cutting board. Using a knife, score the flesh in a cross-hatch pattern. Flip the pork belly over and poke small holes in the skin. Turn the pork belly back over and rub the minced herbs, garlic powder, and salt into the flesh. Place the pork tenderloin in the center of the pork belly and then roll the pork belly up so that it retains its length. Tie the rolled pork belly securely with kitchen twine every ½".

2 Transfer the pork belly to a rack with a large pan underneath, place it in the fridge, and leave uncovered for 2 days. This allows the skin to dry out a bit. Pat the pork belly occasionally with paper towels to remove excess moisture.

3 Remove the pork belly from the refrigerator and let stand at room temperature for 1 to 2 hours. Preheat the oven to 480°F. When the pork belly is room temperature, place the rack and the pan in the oven and cook for 35 minutes, turning to ensure even cooking.

4 Reduce the oven temperature to 300°F and cook until a meat thermometer inserted into the center reaches 145°F, about 1 to 2 hours. The porchetta's skin should be crispy. If it is not as crispy as you'd like, raise the oven's temperature to 500°F and cook until crispy. Remove from the oven and let the porchetta rest for 15 minutes before slicing.

Pork & Apple Casserole

**YIELD: 4 SERVINGS • ACTIVE TIME: 30 MINUTES
TOTAL TIME: 1 HOUR**

When apple season reaches its peak, it's time to lean heavily on this dish.

INGREDIENTS

8 apples, sliced

2 teaspoons cinnamon

1 teaspoon ground nutmeg

¼ cup sugar

¼ cup all-purpose flour

Salt and pepper, to taste

¼ cup apple cider

1½-lb. pork tenderloin

2 tablespoons fresh rosemary
leaves, ground

2 tablespoons fresh thyme
leaves, ground

1 Preheat the oven to 325°F.

2 Place the apples, cinnamon, nutmeg, sugar, flour, and a pinch of salt in a mixing bowl and stir to combine. Transfer the mixture to a baking dish or Dutch oven and then add the apple cider.

3 Rub the pork tenderloin with the ground herbs and a pinch of salt. Place the tenderloin on top of the apple mixture, cover, and place in the oven. Cook until a meat thermometer inserted into the center of the tenderloin registers 145°F, about 40 minutes.

4 Remove the pork tenderloin from the oven and slice. Serve on beds of the apple mixture.

Chipotle Sausage & Peppers

YIELD: 6 SERVINGS • ACTIVE TIME: 15 MINUTES
TOTAL TIME: 4 HOURS

The smoky bite of the chipotle peppers puts a new twist on a ballpark favorite.

1 Place the bell peppers in a slow cooker and set it to high heat. Place the tomatoes, garlic, chipotle peppers, and adobo sauce in a blender and puree until smooth. Pour the puree over the peppers and stir to combine.

2 Add the kielbasa and the habanero to the slow cooker, cover, and cook on high for 4 hours.

3 Discard the habanero. Ladle into warmed bowls or submarine rolls and serve immediately.

INGREDIENTS

5 bell peppers, stemmed, seeded, and sliced

1 (28 oz.) can of tomatoes

3 garlic cloves

2 chipotle peppers en adobo

1 tablespoon abobo sauce

2 lbs. kielbasa, cut into 6 even pieces

1 habanero pepper, pierced

Submarine rolls, for serving (optional)

Pork Fried Rice

YIELD: 8 SERVINGS • ACTIVE TIME: 25 MINUTES
TOTAL TIME: 35 MINUTES

The next time you order Chinese food, add one or two sides of white rice and you'll be halfway home to another delicious meal.

INGREDIENTS

¼ cup olive oil

1 tablespoon minced ginger

2 garlic cloves, minced

1-lb. pork tenderloin, diced

3 large eggs

2 cups minced carrots

4 cups cooked, day-old white rice

4 scallions, chopped

1 cup peas

2 tablespoons soy sauce

1 tablespoon rice vinegar

1 tablespoon fish sauce

1 tablespoon sesame oil

1 Place the oil in a 12" cast-iron skillet and warm over medium-high heat. When the oil starts to shimmer, add the ginger and garlic and cook until they start to brown, about 2 minutes. Raise the heat to high and add the pork. Cook, while stirring, until the pork is well browned, about 5 minutes.

2 Push the pork to one side of the pan and add the eggs. Scramble until the eggs are set, about 2 minutes. Add the carrots, rice, scallions, and peas and stir to incorporate. Add the soy sauce, rice vinegar, fish sauce, and sesame oil and cook, while stirring constantly, for 5 minutes. Serve immediately.

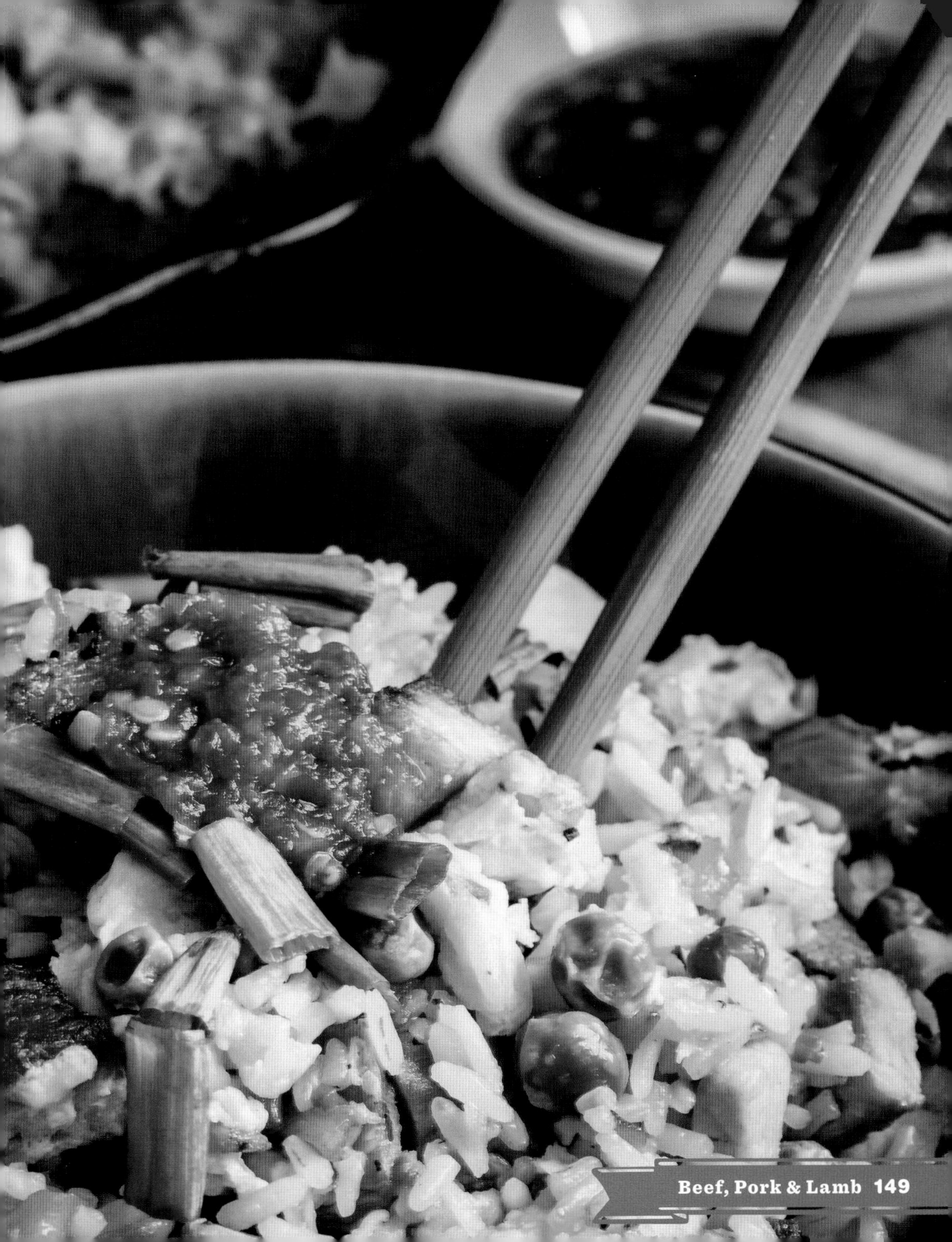

1 lb. ground lamb

1 large yellow onion, diced

2 lbs. red potatoes, peeled and diced

2 lbs. yellow potatoes, peeled and diced

1 tablespoon kosher salt, plus more to taste

1 stick unsalted butter

1 cup half-and-half

3 tablespoons black truffles, minced (optional)

1 cup all-purpose flour

2 cups Beef Stock (see page 12)

2 cups peas

1 cup corn kernels

1 tablespoon soy sauce

1 tablespoon Worcestershire sauce

Shepherd's Pie

YIELD: 4 SERVINGS • ACTIVE TIME: 15 MINUTES
TOTAL TIME: 1½ HOURS

The truffles are a big outlay, but so worth it. Do everything you can to get them into the final product.

1 Preheat the oven to 350°F. Place the lamb in a Dutch oven and cook over medium-high heat, while using a wooden spoon to break it up, until it is brown, about 10 minutes. Drain off the fat, transfer the meat to a bowl, and set aside. Add the onion, cook until it is translucent, and then add to the bowl containing the meat.

2 Wipe out the Dutch oven and add the potatoes and the tablespoon of salt. Cover with water, bring to a boil, and cook until tender, about 20 minutes. Drain, return the potatoes to the Dutch oven, and add the butter, half-and-half, and the truffles, if using. Season with salt

and then mash the potatoes until they are smooth. Place the mashed potatoes in another bowl and set aside.

3 Place the Dutch oven over medium-high heat and add the lamb-and-onion mixture and the flour. Cook, while stirring constantly, for 5 minutes. Add the stock, peas, corn, soy sauce, and Worcestershire sauce and cook, while stirring frequently, until the liquid has reduced by half, 10 to 15 minutes.

4 Place the mashed potatoes on top, use a rubber spatula to even the surface, and then transfer the Dutch oven to the oven. Bake until the pie is hot in the center, about 20 minutes.

Braised Lamb Shoulder

YIELD: 4 SERVINGS • ACTIVE TIME: 30 MINUTES
TOTAL TIME: 4 HOURS

While the lamb is resting, whip up some fresh spring peas, the Marvelous Mushrooms (see page 43), or the Awesome Asparagus (see page 40) in the Dutch oven.

INGREDIENTS

2 tablespoons olive oil

5-lb., bone-in lamb shoulder

Salt, to taste

1 small onion, diced

2 carrots, peeled and diced

3 bay leaves

2 tablespoons
black peppercorns

2 cups water

2 sprigs of rosemary

1 Preheat the oven to 300°F. Place the oil in a Dutch oven and warm it over medium-high heat. Season all sides of the lamb shoulder liberally with salt. When the oil starts to shimmer, place the lamb in the pot and cook, turning occasionally, until it is brown on all sides, about 15 minutes.

2 Add the onion, carrots, bay leaves, peppercorns, water, and rosemary to the Dutch oven, cover it, and place in the oven. Cook until the lamb is fork-tender, approximately 3½ hours. Remove from the oven, transfer to a cutting board, and let it rest for 15 minutes before slicing.

INGREDIENTS

¼ cup olive oil

2 lbs. boneless lamb shoulder, cut into 1" pieces

Salt, to taste

2 large yellow onions, sliced thin

2 tablespoons minced ginger

2 garlic cloves, minced

1 tablespoon curry powder, plus 1 teaspoon

1 teaspoon turmeric

1 teaspoon cayenne pepper, or to taste

1 teaspoon garam masala

1 (14 oz.) can of crushed tomatoes

1 cup plain yogurt

2 cups water

Fresh cilantro, chopped, for garnish

Red onion, diced, for garnish

Rogan Josh

YIELD: 4 SERVINGS • ACTIVE TIME: 20 MINUTES
TOTAL TIME: 1½ HOURS

Pressed for time? This can also be a fantastic make-ahead dish that tastes just as good—if not better—the next day.

1 Place the oil in a Dutch oven and warm over high heat. Season the lamb with salt. When the oil starts to shimmer, add the lamb and cook, turning occasionally, until it is lightly browned all over, about 10 minutes. Remove with a slotted spoon and set aside.

2 Add the onions, ginger, garlic, curry, turmeric, cayenne, and garam masala to the Dutch oven and sauté for 2 minutes.

3 Add the tomatoes, yogurt, and water and bring to a gentle boil. Return the lamb to the pot, lower the heat, cover, and simmer until the lamb is very tender, about 1 hour. Remove the cover occasionally to stir and make sure the rogan josh does not burn.

4 Ladle into warmed bowls and garnish with the cilantro and red onion.

Chicken

As it is the most affordable protein, and the most versatile one due to its neutral flavor, chicken sits at the center of countless recipes. And yet there always seems to be a shortage of enjoyable preparations that utilize it, causing us to fall back on the uninspired standbys our families have seen a thousand times. By putting it into a delectable dumpling (see pages 158–159) and spicing it up in a traditional Indian recipe (see pages 166–167), we show you how to make this bird soar like never before.

INGREDIENTS

2 cups shredded
Napa cabbage

1 teaspoon kosher salt

½ lb. ground chicken

1 tablespoon minced ginger

1 carrot, peeled
and shredded

2 scallions, chopped

2 garlic cloves, minced

2 tablespoons soy sauce

2 teaspoons sesame oil

1 tablespoon
sesame seeds

Large pinch of red
pepper flakes

½ egg, lightly beaten

30 gyoza wrappers

¼ cup olive oil

½ cup water, plus more
as needed

Chicken Gyoza

YIELD: 6 SERVINGS • ACTIVE TIME: 25 MINUTES
TOTAL TIME: 40 MINUTES

Adapted from one of the recipes celebrity chef Ming Tsai built his glittering reputation on.

1 Place the cabbage, salt, chicken, ginger, carrot, scallions, and garlic in a large bowl and stir until thoroughly combined. Add the soy sauce, sesame oil, sesame seeds, red pepper flakes, and egg and stir to incorporate.

2 Place a wrapper on a clean, dry surface. Place 2 teaspoons of the chicken mixture in the center and run a wet finger along the edge of the wrapper. Fold the wrapper into a half-moon and press down on the edge to seal. Repeat until all of the chicken mixture and wrappers have been used.

3 Place a 12" cast-iron skillet over medium-high heat and add 1 tablespoon of the olive oil. Place as many gyoza in the pan as will fit without touching. Add half of the water, cover the pan, and cook until the water has evaporated, about 6 minutes. Turn the gyoza over and cook until crispy, about 1 minute. Transfer to a paper towel–lined plate and repeat until all of the gyoza have been cooked, replenishing the oil and water as needed. Serve immediately.

Buffalo Wings

YIELD: 4 SERVINGS • ACTIVE TIME: 30 MINUTES
TOTAL TIME: 45 MINUTES

The classic we've all come know and love, now in the comfortable confines of the home.

INGREDIENTS

4 tablespoons unsalted butter

1 tablespoon white vinegar

¾ cup hot sauce

1 teaspoon cayenne pepper (optional)

4 cups vegetable oil

2 lbs. chicken wings

1 cup cornstarch

Salt, to taste

Blue Cheese Dressing (see sidebar), for serving

Celery sticks, for serving

1 Place the butter in a Dutch oven and warm over medium heat. When it has melted, whisk in the vinegar, hot sauce, and cayenne (if using), making sure not to breathe in the spicy steam. Transfer the sauce to a mixing bowl and cover to keep warm.

2 Wipe out the Dutch oven, add the vegetable oil, and slowly bring it to 375°F over medium heat. While the oil is heating, pat the wings dry and, working in batches, toss them in the cornstarch.

3 Add the coated wings to the oil in batches and fry until they are crispy, about 10 minutes. Transfer the cooked wings to a wire rack and season with salt. Add the cooked wings to the spicy sauce, toss to coat, and serve them with the Blue Cheese Dressing and celery sticks.

Blue Cheese Dressing

INGREDIENTS

¼ cup sour cream

¼ cup mayonnaise

¼ cup buttermilk

1 tablespoon fresh lemon juice

Pinch of black pepper

1 cup crumbled blue cheese

1 Place the sour cream, mayonnaise, buttermilk, lemon juice, and pepper in a bowl and whisk to combine.

2 Add the blue cheese and stir to incorporate. The dressing will keep in the refrigerator for up to 1 week.

Chicken Kebabs

YIELD: 4 SERVINGS • ACTIVE TIME: 20 MINUTES TOTAL TIME 2½ HOURS

Proof that a simple marinade and a bit of time are all that are needed to produce a delicious dinner.

1 Place the paprika, turmeric, onion powder, garlic powder, oregano, olive oil, vinegar, yogurt, and salt in a large bowl and whisk to combine. Add the chicken pieces and stir until they are coated. Cover the bowl and let the chicken marinate for at least 2 hours. If you have time, you can also let the chicken marinate overnight.

2 Place a cast-iron grill pan or skillet over medium-high heat and warm for 10 minutes. While the pan is heating up, thread the chicken onto the skewers and season with salt and pepper.

3 Brush the pan with a light coating of olive oil and then add the chicken kebabs. Cook, while turning occasionally, until the chicken is golden brown and cooked through, approximately 10 minutes. Serve warm or at room temperature with the lemon wedges.

INGREDIENTS

2 tablespoons paprika

1 teaspoon turmeric

1 teaspoon onion powder

1 teaspoon garlic powder

1 tablespoon dried oregano

¼ cup olive oil, plus more as needed

2 tablespoons white wine vinegar

1 cup plain Greek yogurt

1 teaspoon kosher salt, plus more to taste

3 lbs. boneless, skinless chicken thighs, cut into bite-sized pieces

Metal or wooden skewers

Black pepper, to taste

Lemon wedges, for serving

Chicken Fajitas

YIELD: 6 SERVINGS • ACTIVE TIME: 30 MINUTES
TOTAL TIME: 5 HOURS

The trick is to bring this dish to the table while the meat and veggies are still sizzling, as the sound is sure to get mouths watering.

1 To begin preparations for the chicken, place the orange juice, lime juice, garlic, jalapeño, cilantro, cumin, oregano, salt, and pepper in a bowl and stir to combine. When thoroughly combined, add the olive oil. Add the chicken pieces to the mixture, stir until they are evenly coated, cover with plastic wrap, and refrigerate for about 4 hours.

2 Place a 12" cast-iron skillet over medium-high heat. Add the chicken and cook, while stirring, until browned and cooked through. Transfer the chicken to a bowl and tent loosely with foil to keep warm.

3 To prepare the vegetables, reduce the heat to medium, add the olive oil to the skillet, and then add the onion, peppers, and garlic. Cook, while stirring, until the vegetables have softened, about 5 minutes. Add the lime juice and cilantro, season with salt and pepper, and cook until the vegetables are tender, about 10 minutes.

4 Push the vegetables to one side of the pan and put the chicken on the other side. Serve immediately with the Corn Tortillas, Guacamole, and pico de gallo.

INGREDIENTS
For the Chicken

½ cup orange juice

Juice of 1 lime

4 garlic cloves, minced

1 jalapeño pepper, stemmed, seeded, and diced

2 tablespoons chopped fresh cilantro

1 teaspoon cumin

1 teaspoon dried oregano

Salt and pepper, to taste

3 tablespoons olive oil

4 boneless, skinless chicken breasts, cut into strips

For the Vegetables

2 tablespoons olive oil

1 red onion, sliced thin

1 red bell pepper, stemmed, seeded, and sliced thin

1 green bell pepper, stemmed, seeded, and sliced thin

1 yellow bell pepper, stemmed, seeded, and sliced thin

2 jalapeño peppers, stemmed, seeded, and sliced thin

3 garlic cloves, minced

¼ cup fresh lime juice

½ cup chopped fresh cilantro

Salt and pepper, to taste

For Serving

Corn Tortillas (see page 23)

Guacamole (see page 28)

Pico de gallo (see pages 62–63)

INGREDIENTS

1 tablespoon garam masala

1 teaspoon turmeric

2 teaspoons sweet paprika

1 teaspoon mustard powder

2 tablespoons sugar

1 teaspoon cumin

Cayenne pepper, to taste

½ cup red wine vinegar

¼ cup tomato paste

5 tablespoons olive oil

4-lb. chicken, cut
into pieces

1 large yellow onion, sliced

6 garlic cloves, minced

1 tablespoon minced ginger

1 (14 oz.) can of chopped
tomatoes, drained

Fresh cilantro, chopped,
for garnish

Chicken Vindaloo

YIELD: 6 SERVINGS • ACTIVE TIME: 30 MINUTES
TOTAL TIME: 2½ HOURS

A word of advice: add as much cayenne pepper as you and your family can handle, as this beloved preparation improves as it gets spicier.

1 Place the garam masala, turmeric, paprika, mustard powder, sugar, cumin, cayenne pepper, vinegar, tomato paste, and 2 tablespoons of the olive oil in a mixing bowl and stir to combine. Add the chicken to the mixture, turn until the pieces are evenly coated, cover the bowl, and place it in the refrigerator for 2 hours. If time allows, let the chicken marinate overnight.

2 Place a Dutch oven over high heat and add the remaining oil. When the oil starts to shimmer, add the onion and cook until it is translucent, about 3 minutes. Reduce the heat to medium, add the garlic and ginger, and sauté for 1 minute.

3 Add the tomatoes, chicken, and the marinade to the pot and bring to a boil. Reduce the heat and simmer until the chicken is cooked through, about 18 minutes. Garnish with the cilantro and serve.

Pad Thai

**YIELD: 4 SERVINGS • ACTIVE TIME: 15 MINUTES
TOTAL TIME: 35 MINUTES**

The key to this recipe is balancing the flavors properly so that you have a tangle of chewy noodles freighted with a delicious jumble of salty, sweet, sour, and spicy.

INGREDIENTS

6 oz. thin rice noodles

3 tablespoons olive oil

3 chicken breasts, sliced thin

1 large egg

¼ cup tamarind paste

2 tablespoons water

1½ tablespoons fish sauce

2 tablespoons rice vinegar

1½ tablespoons brown sugar

4 scallion greens, sliced

1 cup bean sprouts

½ teaspoon cayenne pepper

¼ cup crushed peanuts

Lime wedges, for serving

1 Place the noodles in a bowl and cover them with boiling water. Stir and let rest until they have softened, about 15 minutes.

2 Place the oil in a 12" cast-iron skillet and warm over medium-high heat. When the oil starts to shimmer, add the chicken and cook until cooked through, about 5 minutes. Remove the chicken from the pan and set aside.

3 Add the egg and stir. Add the noodles and return the chicken to the pan. Stir to incorporate and then add the tamarind paste, water, fish sauce, vinegar, brown sugar, scallions, bean sprouts, cayenne pepper, and peanuts. Stir to combine and serve immediately with the lime wedges.

INGREDIENTS

1 yellow onion, chopped

10 garlic cloves, peeled and trimmed

2 scotch bonnet peppers, stemmed, seeded, and chopped

1 cup chopped fresh cilantro

1 teaspoon dried thyme

1 tablespoon cumin

½ teaspoon allspice

1 cup orange juice

½ cup fresh lemon juice

½ teaspoon citric acid (optional)

Zest and juice of 1 lime

¼ cup olive oil

Salt and pepper, to taste

4 boneless, skinless chicken breasts

Mojo Chicken

**YIELD: 4 SERVINGS • ACTIVE TIME: 30 MINUTES
TOTAL TIME: 2½ HOURS**

This fiery, Cuban-inspired dish will wake up your family's taste buds every time.

1 Place all of the ingredients, except for the chicken, in a food processor or blender and puree until smooth. Reserve ½ cup of the marinade, pour the rest into a large resealable plastic bag, and add the chicken. Place in the refrigerator and marinate for 2 hours. If time allows, let the chicken marinate for up to 8 hours.

2 Warm a grill pan over very high heat. Remove the chicken from the marinade and pat dry. When the pan is hot, add the chicken and cook until both sides are charred and the breasts are cooked through, about 4 minutes per side.

3 Remove the chicken from the pan, transfer it to a plate, and tent loosely with foil to keep warm. Add the reserved marinade to the pan. Reduce the heat to medium and simmer the marinade until it starts to thicken. Spoon it over the chicken and serve immediately.

Shredded Chicken with Beans & Rice

YIELD: 6 SERVINGS • ACTIVE TIME: 10 MINUTES
TOTAL TIME: 5 TO 6 HOURS

The cumin provides earthiness, the jalapeño provides a bit of heat, and they combine to add depth to what should be a simple bowl of chicken and rice.

1 Place the chicken, stock, jalapeño, garlic, cumin, and granulated garlic in a slow cooker and cook on high until the chicken is very tender and falling apart, about 4 hours. Remove the chicken, place it in a bowl, and shred it with a fork.

2 Add the rice, tomatoes, salt, and pepper to the slow cooker and cook until the rice is tender, about 1 hour. Make sure to check the rice for doneness after 45 minutes, since cook times will vary between different brands of slow cookers.

3 Add the black beans, stir to combine, top with the shredded chicken, and cover to warm everything through. Garnish with additional jalapeño before serving.

INGREDIENTS

6 boneless, skinless chicken breasts

1 cup Chicken Stock (see page 11)

1 jalapeño pepper, stemmed, seeded, and minced, plus more for garnish

2 garlic cloves, minced

1½ tablespoons cumin

1 tablespoon granulated garlic

1 cup white rice

2 plum tomatoes, diced

2 tablespoons kosher salt

1 tablespoon black pepper

1 (14 oz.) can of black beans, drained

Chicken & Sausage Cacciatore

YIELD: 6 SERVINGS • ACTIVE TIME: 10 MINUTES
TOTAL TIME: 6 HOURS AND 15 MINUTES

Tender chicken thighs, sweet Italian sausage, earthy oregano, and salty Parmesan combine to create a mouthwatering main course.

1 Place all of the ingredients, save the white rice and the Parmesan, in a slow cooker and cook on low for 5½ hours.

2 Add the rice to the slow cooker, raise the heat to high, and cook until the rice is tender, about 1 hour. The cooking time may vary depending on your slow cooker, so be sure to check after about 45 minutes to avoid overcooking the rice.

3 Top with a generous amount of Parmesan cheese and serve immediately.

INGREDIENTS

1 lb. sweet Italian sausage

6 boneless, skinless chicken thighs

1 (28 oz.) can of whole San Marzano tomatoes

1 (28 oz.) can of diced tomatoes

⅔ cup dry red wine

4 shallots, diced

3 garlic cloves, minced

1 green bell pepper, stemmed, seeded, and diced

1 yellow bell pepper, stemmed, seeded, and diced

3 tablespoons dried oregano

1 tablespoon granulated garlic

1 tablespoon sugar

2 tablespoons kosher salt, plus more to taste

½ teaspoon red pepper flakes

Black pepper, to taste

1 cup white rice

Parmesan cheese, grated, for garnish

Caprese Chicken

YIELD: 6 SERVINGS • ACTIVE TIME: 15 MINUTES
TOTAL TIME: 45 MINUTES

By tossing a traditional caprese salad between layers of thinly sliced chicken breast, you transform a ho-hum set of ingredients into a dazzling dinner.

1 Preheat the oven to 375°F. Place the garlic, oregano, granulated garlic, salt, and pepper in a bowl and stir to combine. Place 1 tablespoon of the olive oil and the sliced chicken breasts in a bowl and toss to coat. Dredge the chicken breasts in the garlic-and-seasoning mixture and set aside.

2 Coat the bottom of a 12" cast-iron skillet with the remaining oil and warm over medium-high heat. Working in batches, sear the chicken breasts for 1 minute on each side.

3 When all of the chicken has been seared, place half of the breasts in an even layer on the bottom of the skillet. Top with two-thirds of the tomatoes and mozzarella, and half of the basil leaves. Place the remaining chicken breasts on top and cover with the remaining tomatoes, mozzarella, and basil.

4 Place the skillet in the oven and cook until the interior temperature of the chicken breasts is 165°F, about 10 minutes. Remove the skillet from the oven and let rest for 10 minutes. Drizzle the balsamic glaze over the top and serve.

INGREDIENTS

1 garlic clove, minced

1 teaspoon dried oregano

1 teaspoon granulated garlic

Salt and pepper, to taste

2 tablespoons olive oil

6 boneless, skinless chicken
breasts, halved along
their equator

2 lbs. plum tomatoes, sliced

1 lb. fresh mozzarella cheese,
sliced into ¼" pieces

Leaves from 1 bunch of basil

Balsamic glaze, for garnish

INGREDIENTS

⅓ cup olive oil, plus
2 tablespoons

6 skin-on chicken legs

1 tablespoon kosher salt,
plus more to taste

1 tablespoon black pepper,
plus more to taste

5 shallots, diced

3 garlic cloves, minced

2 red potatoes, diced

4 Yukon Gold potatoes,
peeled and chopped

3 fennel bulbs, diced,
fronds reserved for garnish

1 teaspoon celery seeds

1 teaspoon fennel seeds

½ cup sun-dried tomatoes

1 cup Chardonnay

6 tablespoons
unsalted butter

Chicken Legs with Potatoes & Fennel

YIELD: 6 SERVINGS • ACTIVE TIME: 30 MINUTES
TOTAL TIME: 1 HOUR

Turn to this one when you need some comfort, it's likely to stick with you for a while.

1 Place a Dutch oven over medium-high heat and add the ⅓ cup of olive oil. Rub the chicken legs with the remaining oil and season with the salt and pepper. When the oil starts to shimmer, add half of the chicken legs to the pot, skin-side down, and cook until the skin is golden brown and crusted, about 5 minutes. Remove, set aside, and repeat with the remaining chicken legs.

2 Preheat the oven to 400°F. Add the shallots and garlic to the Dutch oven and use a wooden spoon to scrape all of the browned bits from the bottom. Cook until the shallots and garlic darken, about 2 minutes. Raise the heat to high and add the remaining ingredients, except for the wine and the butter. Cook, while stirring occasionally, for about 15 minutes.

3 Add the wine and the butter, stir, and then return the chicken to the pan, skin-side up. Reduce the heat, cover, and cook until the potatoes are tender and the chicken is 155°F in the center, about 30 minutes. Remove the lid, transfer the Dutch oven to the oven, and cook until the chicken is 165°F in the center. Garnish with the fennel fronds and serve.

Jerk Chicken with Vegetables

**YIELD: 6 SERVINGS • ACTIVE TIME: 15 MINUTES
TOTAL TIME: 24 HOURS**

By substituting root vegetables for the rice and beans that are traditionally served with jerk chicken, you add extra nutrition to this legendary dish.

1 To prepare the marinade, place all of the ingredients in a blender and puree until smooth. Pour the marinade over the chicken and refrigerate overnight.

2 To prepare the chicken and vegetables, preheat the oven to 375°F. Place the vegetables, olive oil, salt, and pepper in a 9 x 13-inch baking pan and roast for 30 minutes. Remove, add the thyme, return the pan to the oven, and cook for an additional 25 minutes.

3 Remove the pan from the oven. Shake the chicken to remove any excess marinade and then place the chicken on top of the vegetables. Return the pan to the oven and cook for 45 to 50 minutes, until the interiors of thickest parts of the chicken reach 165°F. Remove the pan from the oven and serve immediately.

INGREDIENTS

For the Marinade

2 tablespoons fresh thyme leaves

2 habanero peppers, stemmed and seeded, or to taste

½ yellow onion

½ cup brown sugar

½ tablespoon cinnamon

½ teaspoon ground nutmeg

1 tablespoon allspice

2 tablespoons minced ginger

1 cup canola oil (or preferred neutral oil)

2 tablespoons soy sauce

1 scallion

1 tablespoon kosher salt

1 tablespoon black pepper

1 tablespoon rice vinegar

For the Chicken & Vegetables

5 lbs. bone-in, skin-on chicken pieces

3 red beets, peeled and diced

3 carrots, peeled and diced

1 large sweet potato, peeled and diced

3 turnips, peeled and diced

¼ cup olive oil

Salt and pepper, to taste

2 tablespoons fresh thyme leaves, chopped

6 bone-in, skin-on chicken breasts

¼ cup red wine

1 cup sliced mushrooms

¼ cup Chicken Stock (see page 11)

½ lb. no-boil lasagna sheets, broken into pieces

4 plum tomatoes, diced

1 cup chopped beet greens, rinsed well

8 to 10 pepperoncini, halved lengthwise

1 cup Asiago cheese, shredded, plus more for garnish

1 tablespoon dried oregano

1 teaspoon garlic powder

½ teaspoon red pepper flakes

Zest and juice of 1 lemon

Salt and pepper, to taste

Fresh basil, chopped, for garnish

Baked Chicken & Pasta

YIELD: 6 SERVINGS • ACTIVE TIME: 30 MINUTES
TOTAL TIME: 2 HOURS

The best part of this meal is the lovely balance struck by the sweet pepperoncini and the earthy flavor of the mushrooms.

1 Preheat the oven to 375°F. Place the chicken breasts, red wine, mushrooms, and stock in a 9 x 13-inch baking pan and bake for 45 minutes, until the internal temperature of the chicken is 150°F.

2 Remove the baking pan from the oven, remove the chicken from the baking pan, and let rest for 10 minutes. Remove the skin and bones from the chicken and discard. Tear the chicken into large chunks and return it to the pan.

3 Add the lasagna sheets, tomatoes, beet greens, pepperoncini, Asiago, oregano, garlic powder, red pepper flakes, lemon zest, lemon juice, salt, and pepper to the baking pan. Top with additional Asiago, place the pan in the oven, and bake until the pasta is tender and the mixture in the pan is bubbling, about 40 minutes. Remove the pan from the oven, garnish with fresh basil, and serve.

Chicken & Tomatillo Casserole

YIELD: 6 SERVINGS • ACTIVE TIME: 15 MINUTES
TOTAL TIME: 24 HOURS

Packed with shredded chicken and tangy tomatillos, this is what lasagna might have been had it been created in the American Southwest.

1 To prepare the marinade, place all of the ingredients in a blender and puree until smooth. Pour the marinade over the chicken breasts and refrigerate overnight.

2 Preheat the oven to 375°F. Place the chicken and marinade in a square 8" baking dish, place it in the oven, and cook until the center of the chicken reaches 155°F, about 25 minutes. Remove the dish from the oven, remove the chicken, transfer it to a mixing bowl, and shred it with a fork. Add the eggs, tomatoes, and salt and stir to combine.

3 Place four of the tortillas in the baking dish. Add half of the chicken mixture, top with four more tortillas, and add the remaining chicken mixture. Top with remaining tortillas, cover with the Salsa Verde, and then place the dish in the oven. Bake for about 30 minutes, until the center is hot. Remove, sprinkle the cheese on top, and return to the oven. Bake until the cheese has melted, remove, and serve.

INGREDIENTS
For the Marinade

1 tomatillo, husked, rinsed, and halved

1 plum tomato, halved

2 garlic cloves

1 shallot, halved

1 poblano pepper, stemmed, seeded, and halved

¼ cup olive oil

1 tablespoon kosher salt

1 tablespoon cumin

For the Casserole

6 boneless, skinless chicken breasts, sliced thin

2 eggs, beaten

1 (14 oz.) can of fire-roasted tomatoes

Pinch of kosher salt

14 corn tortillas (see page 23 for homemade)

1 cup Salsa Verde (see page 27)

¼ cup crumbled Cotija cheese

Seafood

The world's oceans are the biggest sources of food on the planet, and the fast cook times seafood's unparalleled freshness enable make it a major boon to the busy cook. But as most parents know, not everyone is eager to dive in. With that in mind, we selected dishes that present the fruits of the sea in flavorful packages that all ages will find agreeable, while also embracing the ease and speed that make the incredible bounty provided by the sea such a crucial part of the contemporary kitchen.

Fish & Chips

YIELD: 4 SERVINGS • ACTIVE TIME: 20 MINUTES
TOTAL TIME: 45 MINUTES

Pollock has a similar flavor to cod, and is a far more sustainable choice for this classic dish.

INGREDIENTS

4 cups canola oil

5 potatoes, sliced into long, thin strips

3 tablespoons fresh rosemary leaves, chopped

Salt, to taste

2 eggs, beaten

1 cup cornmeal

1½ lbs. pollock fillets

2 eggs, beaten

1 Place the oil in a Dutch oven and bring to 350°F over medium-high heat.

2 When the oil is ready, place the sliced potatoes in the oil and cook until golden brown. Remove and set to drain on a paper towel–lined plate. Keep the oil at 350°F.

3 Place the fried potatoes in a bowl with the rosemary and salt and toss to coat. Set aside.

4 Place the beaten eggs in a small bowl and the cornmeal in another. Dip the pollock fillets into the egg and then into the cornmeal, repeating until they are coated all over. Place the battered pollock in the oil and cook until golden brown. Remove and set to drain on another paper towel–lined plate. Serve with the fried potatoes.

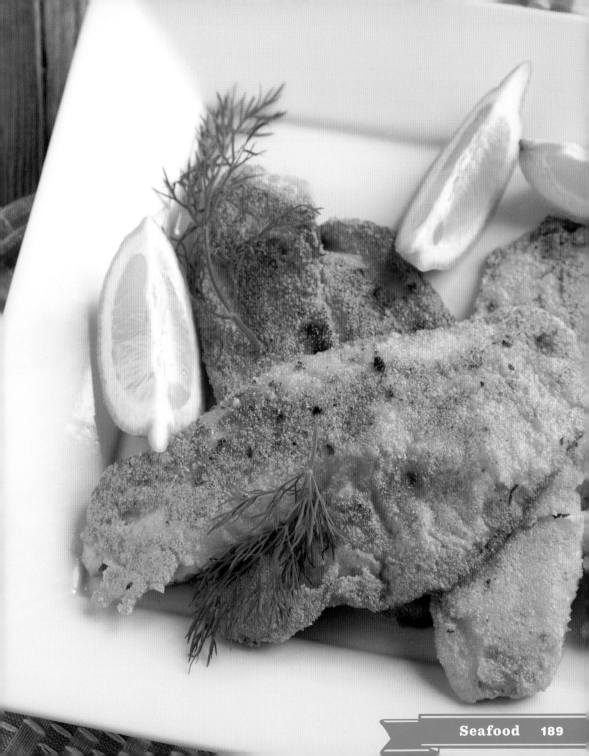

INGREDIENTS

For the Teriyaki Sauce

1 tablespoon minced ginger

3 garlic cloves, minced

1 tablespoon rice vinegar

2 tablespoons brown sugar

¼ cup soy sauce

1 tablespoon tapioca starch or cornstarch

½ cup water

For the Salmon & Vegetables

3 tablespoons olive oil

4 Chinese eggplants, sliced into ½" pieces

1 red bell pepper, stemmed, seeded, and sliced thin

2 tablespoons chopped scallions

1 cup bean sprouts

1½ lbs. salmon fillets

Salt and pepper, to taste

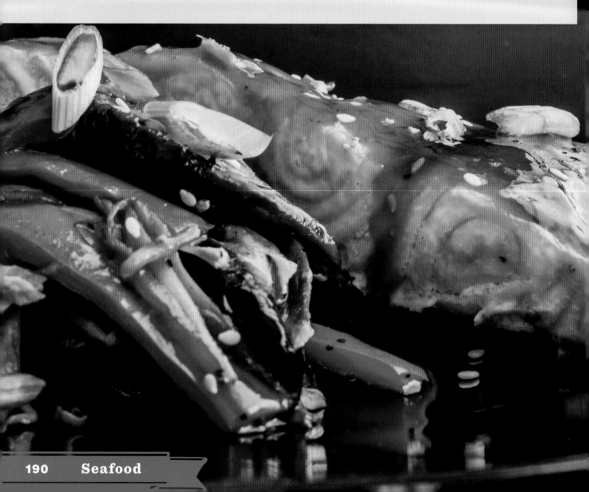

Teriyaki Salmon & Vegetables

YIELD: 4 SERVINGS • ACTIVE TIME: 20 MINUTES
TOTAL TIME: 20 MINUTES

A great starting place if you've got a family full of folks who are wary of seafood.

1 To prepare the teriyaki sauce, place all of the ingredients in a blender and puree until smooth. Transfer to a 12" cast-iron skillet and cook, while stirring, over medium heat until the sauce starts to thicken. Remove from heat and set aside.

2 Wipe out the skillet and preheat the oven to 375°F. To begin preparations for the salmon and vegetables, place the olive oil in the skillet and warm over medium-high heat. Add the eggplants, bell pepper, and scallions to the pan and cook, while stirring occasionally, until the eggplants start to break down, about 5 minutes. Add the bean sprouts and stir to incorporate.

3 Place the salmon on the vegetables, skin-side down, season with salt, pepper, and some of the teriyaki sauce, and transfer the pan to the oven. Cook for 8 to 10 minutes, remove the pan from the oven, top with more teriyaki sauce, and serve.

Halibut with Braised Vegetables

**YIELD: 4 SERVINGS • ACTIVE TIME: 30 MINUTES
TOTAL TIME: 1 HOUR**

The kale is key to this one, as it provides a nice soft bed for the halibut and ensures that it remains moist and full of flavor.

1 Place the olive oil in a Dutch oven and warm over medium-high heat. When the oil starts to shimmer, add the bell peppers, habanero pepper, sweet potatoes, and cabbage. Season with salt and pepper and cook, while stirring, until the sweet potatoes begin to caramelize, about 6 minutes.

2 Add the eggplants, ginger, and garlic and cook, while stirring frequently, until the eggplants begin to break down, about 10 minutes. Add the curry paste and stir to coat all of the vegetables. Cook until the mixture is fragrant, about 2 minutes.

3 Add the bok choy, stock, paprika, cilantro, and coconut milk and cook until the liquid has been reduced by one-quarter, about 20 minutes.

4 Add the kale to the Dutch oven. Place the halibut fillets on top of the kale, reduce the heat to medium, cover, and cook for about 10 minutes, or until the fish is cooked through.

5 Remove the Dutch oven's cover and discard the habanero. Ladle the vegetables and the sauce into the bowls and top each one with a halibut fillet. Garnish with the scallions and serve.

INGREDIENTS

¼ cup olive oil

1 yellow bell pepper, stemmed, seeded, and diced

1 red bell pepper, stemmed, seeded, and diced

1 habanero pepper, pierced

2 small white sweet potatoes, peeled and diced

1 cup diced red cabbage

Salt and pepper, to taste

3 graffiti eggplants, cut into 2" pieces

2 tablespoons mashed ginger

4 garlic cloves, minced

2 tablespoons green curry paste

3 baby bok choy, chopped

4 cups Fish Stock (see page 15)

2 tablespoons sweet paprika

2 tablespoons chopped fresh cilantro

3 (14 oz.) cans of coconut milk

2 bunches of Tuscan kale, stems removed, leaves torn

1½ lbs. halibut fillets

Scallions, chopped, for garnish

Cajun Tilapia

YIELD: 4 SERVINGS • ACTIVE TIME: 5 MINUTES
TOTAL TIME: 15 MINUTES

Tilapia is wonderful for blackening, as it is a firm-fleshed fish that is fairly bland and thus benefits from generous seasoning and a bit of char.

1 Place the seasonings in a bowl, stir to combine, and set aside. Place the melted butter in a separate bowl.

2 Warm a 12" cast-iron skillet over high heat until it is extremely hot, about 10 minutes. While the skillet heats up, rinse the fillets and then pat dry with paper towels. Dip the fillets in the melted butter, covering both sides, and then press the blackened seasoning generously into both sides.

3 Place the fillets in the skillet and cook until cooked through, about 3 minutes per side. Baste the fillets with any remaining butter as they cook. Serve with lemon wedges.

INGREDIENTS

2 tablespoons paprika

1 tablespoon onion powder

3 tablespoons garlic powder

2 tablespoons cayenne pepper

1½ teaspoons celery salt

1½ tablespoons black pepper

1 tablespoon dried thyme

1 tablespoon dried oregano

1 tablespoon chipotle powder

1 stick unsalted butter, melted

4 (4 oz.) boneless tilapia fillets

Lemon wedges, for serving

Red Snapper with Tomatillo Sauce

YIELD: 4 SERVINGS • ACTIVE TIME: 10 MINUTES
TOTAL TIME: 10 MINUTES

This recipe comes together in under 15 minutes, but it's still as joyous and awe-inspiring as a fireworks show on the Fourth of July.

INGREDIENTS

1 lb. tomatillos, husked, rinsed, and quartered

½ white onion, chopped

1 serrano pepper, stemmed

1 garlic clove, crushed

1 bunch of fresh cilantro, some leaves reserved for garnish

2 tablespoons olive oil

1½ lbs. skinless red snapper fillets

Radish, sliced, for garnish

Guacamole (see page 28), for serving

Corn tortillas (see page 23 for homemade), for serving

Lime wedges, for serving

1 Place a dry 12" cast-iron skillet over high heat and add the tomatillos, onion, and serrano pepper. Cook until the tomatillos and pepper are charred slightly, about 5 minutes, and then transfer them to a blender. Add the garlic and cilantro and puree until smooth.

2 Place the oil in the skillet and warm over medium-high heat. When the oil starts to shimmer, add the red snapper fillets in a single layer and cook until they start to brown. Do not turn them over.

3 Remove the pan from heat and allow it to cool for a few minutes. Carefully pour the tomatillo sauce over the fish. It will immediately start to simmer. Place the skillet over medium heat and let it simmer until the fish is cooked through, about 4 minutes. Garnish with the reserved cilantro and sliced radish and serve with the Guacamole, tortillas, and lime wedges.

INGREDIENTS

1 lb. lump crabmeat (blue crab preferred)

¼ cup minced yellow onion

½ cup bread crumbs

1 teaspoon Worcestershire sauce

1 teaspoon Old Bay seasoning

2 tablespoons hot sauce

1 teaspoon dried parsley

1 tablespoon mayonnaise, plus more as needed

1 tablespoon whole milk

1 large egg, lightly beaten

Salt and pepper, to taste

¼ cup olive oil

Lemon wedges, for serving

Carolina Crab Cakes

YIELD: 4 SERVINGS • ACTIVE TIME: 40 MINUTES
TOTAL TIME: 40 MINUTES

Avoid canned crabmeat, as it has neither the flavor nor the consistency needed for these cakes.

1 Place the crabmeat, onion, bread crumbs, Worcestershire sauce, Old Bay seasoning, hot sauce, parsley, and mayonnaise in a mixing bowl and stir to combine. Add the milk and egg and stir until thoroughly incorporated. Season with salt and pepper. If mix seems too dry, add some more mayonnaise.

2 Place a 12" cast-iron skillet over medium-high heat. Add the oil. It should be about ¼" deep. When oil is hot, add 4 heaping spoonfuls of the crab mixture to the skillet, pressing down on the top of each one to form a patty. Brown the cakes on each side for about 3 minutes. Try to turn the cakes over just once. If you're worried about them not getting cooked through, put a lid on the skillet for a minute or so after they've browned on each side.

3 Transfer the cakes to a plate and tent loosely with foil to keep them warm while you cook the next batch. Serve on a platter with lemon wedges on the side.

Thai Mussels

YIELD: 4 SERVINGS • ACTIVE TIME: 15 MINUTES
TOTAL TIME: 25 MINUTES

The combination of sweet, sour, and spicy that Thai cuisine is famous for is on full display in this delightful and flavorful dish.

1 Wash the mussels thoroughly and discard any that aren't tightly closed. Remove the cilantro leaves from the stems. Set the leaves aside and finely chop the stems.

2 Place the olive oil in a Dutch oven and warm over medium-high heat until it is shimmering. Add the shallots, garlic, chopped cilantro stems, lemongrass, and the bird's eye chili and cook, while stirring, until the garlic is lightly browned, about 2 minutes. Add the coconut milk and, if using, the fish sauce and bring to a boil.

3 Add the mussels and immediately cover the pot. Steam the mussels until the majority of them have opened and the meat is still plump, about 5 minutes. Be careful not to overcook the mussels, as it will cause them to have a rubbery texture. Discard any mussels that do not open.

4 Stir a few times to coat the mussels and add half of the lime juice. Taste and add more lime juice as needed. Ladle into warmed bowls and garnish with the reserved cilantro leaves.

INGREDIENTS

2 lbs. mussels, debearded

½ cup fresh cilantro

1 tablespoon olive oil

4 shallots, minced

2 garlic cloves, sliced

1 lemongrass stalk, cut into 4 large pieces

1 bird's eye chili pepper, stemmed, seeded to taste, and sliced

1 (14 oz.) can of coconut milk

1 tablespoon fish sauce (optional)

Juice of 1 lime

INGREDIENTS

16 large shrimp, shelled and deveined

1 cup shredded unsweetened coconut

1 teaspoon cumin seeds

3 chiles de árbol, stemmed

2 large tomatoes, chopped

¼ cup olive oil

5 whole cloves

4 green cardamom pods

2 bay leaves

1 cinnamon stick

1 yellow onion, chopped

1 tablespoon ground coriander

1 teaspoon turmeric

1 teaspoon black pepper

2 garlic cloves, mashed

1 teaspoon mashed ginger

1 (14 oz.) can of coconut milk

½ cup water

2 tablespoons brown sugar

2 serrano peppers, stemmed, seeded, and sliced thin

1 cup fresh cilantro, chopped

Salt, to taste

Shrimp Curry

**YIELD: 4 SERVINGS • ACTIVE TIME: 10 MINUTES
TOTAL TIME: 20 MINUTES**

Once you see how much flavor this has and how quickly it's ready, you won't even bat an eye when confronted by this long list of ingredients.

1 Place four of the shrimp, the coconut, cumin seeds, chiles de árbol, tomatoes, and olive oil in a food processor and puree until the mixture is a paste.

2 Place the cloves, cardamom pods, bay leaves, and cinnamon stick in a dry 12" cast-iron skillet and cook over medium heat until fragrant, about 1 minute. Stir in the onion, coriander, turmeric, black pepper, garlic, and ginger. Cook for 1 minute, add the shrimp paste, and stir to combine. Cook, while stirring often, for 4 minutes.

3 Add the coconut milk and water and bring to a boil. Add the brown sugar and serrano peppers, stir to incorporate, and cook for another minute.

4 Reduce the heat, add the remaining shrimp and the cilantro, and simmer until the shrimp are pink and the sauce thickens slightly, 6 to 8 minutes. Season with salt and ladle into warmed bowls.

TIP: FOR A MORE AUTHENTIC PREPARATION, SUBSTITUTE JAGGERY, AN UNREFINED SUGAR THAT TYPICALLY COMES FROM THE SAP OF PALM TREES, FOR THE BROWN SUGAR.

Garlic Shrimp

YIELD: 4 SERVINGS • ACTIVE TIME: 5 MINUTES
TOTAL TIME: 10 MINUTES

What's not to like here? Sweet, briny shrimp, loads of luscious butter, and a bit of mellowed garlic, all held together by the acidic kick of lemon.

INGREDIENTS

4 tablespoons unsalted butter, at room temperature

1 lb. shrimp, shelled and deveined

8 garlic cloves, minced

½ teaspoon lemon-pepper seasoning

1 tablespoon fresh lemon juice

1 teaspoon minced chives or parsley, for garnish

1 red chili pepper, stemmed, seeded, and sliced thin, for garnish

1 Place a 10" cast-iron skillet over medium heat and add the butter.

2 When the butter has melted and is foaming, add the shrimp and cook, without stirring, for 3 minutes. Remove the shrimp from the pan with a slotted spoon and set them aside.

3 Reduce the heat to medium-low and add the garlic and lemon-pepper seasoning. Cook until the garlic has softened, about 4 minutes. Return the shrimp to the pan and cook, while stirring, until warmed through, about 1 minute. To serve, sprinkle with the lemon juice and garnish with the chives or parsley and the sliced chili pepper.

INGREDIENTS

½ lb. andouille
sausage, sliced

½ lb. small shrimp, shelled
and deveined

¼ cup olive oil

4 boneless, skinless chicken
thighs, cut into 2" pieces

2 yellow onions, diced

1 large green bell pepper,
stemmed, seeded, and diced

2 celery stalks, diced

3 garlic cloves, minced

2 to 3 plum tomatoes, diced

2 bay leaves

2 tablespoons paprika

2 tablespoons dried thyme

1 tablespoon granulated garlic

1 tablespoon granulated onion

1 teaspoon cayenne pepper

1½ cups long-grain white rice

2 tablespoons
Worcestershire sauce

Hot sauce, to taste

3 cups Chicken Stock
(see page 11)

Salt and pepper, to taste

Scallions, chopped,
for garnish

Jambalaya

**YIELD: 6 SERVINGS • ACTIVE TIME: 25 MINUTES
TOTAL TIME: 1 HOUR AND 15 MINUTES**

Charring the sausages at the beginning of your preparation adds an indispensable smokiness to this Cajun classic.

1 Place the sausage in a Dutch oven and cook over medium-high heat. Cook for 2 minutes on each side, remove, and set aside. Add the shrimp and cook for 1 minute on each side. Remove and set aside.

2 Add the oil, chicken, onions, bell pepper, and celery. Cook until the vegetables start to caramelize and the chicken is browned and cooked through, 6 to 8 minutes. Add the garlic and cook for another 2 minutes.

3 Add the tomatoes, the bay leaves, and all of the seasonings. Cook for 30 minutes and stir occasionally to prevent the contents of the Dutch oven from burning.

4 Add the rice, Worcestershire sauce, hot sauce, and stock. Return the sausage to the pot, reduce heat to medium-low, cover, and cook for 25 minutes.

5 Return the shrimp to the pot, cover, and cook for 5 minutes. Season with salt and pepper, ladle into warmed bowls, and garnish with the scallions.

Linguine with Clam Sauce

YIELD: 6 SERVINGS • ACTIVE TIME: 20 MINUTES
TOTAL TIME: 40 MINUTES

If you don't have much time but want to bring something special to the table, this dish won't let you down.

1 Bring water to a boil in a Dutch oven. Add the linguine and the salt and cook until the pasta is just short of al dente, about 7 minutes. Drain, while reserving ¼ cup of cooking water, and set the linguine aside.

2 Place the Dutch oven over medium heat. Add half of the olive oil and the garlic to the pot and cook until the garlic starts to brown, about 2 minutes. Add the clams and wine, cover, and cook until the majority of the clams have opened, about 7 minutes. Use a slotted spoon to transfer the clams to a colander. Discard any clams that do not open.

3 Add the clam juice, parsley, and pasta water to the Dutch oven. Cook until the sauce starts to thicken, about 10 minutes. Remove all of the meat from the clams and mince one-quarter of it.

4 Return the linguine to the pot. Add the Parmesan, season with salt and pepper, and stir until the cheese begins to melt. Fold in the clam meat, drizzle with the remaining olive oil, and serve.

INGREDIENTS

1 lb. linguine

2 tablespoons kosher salt,
plus more to taste

½ cup olive oil

3 garlic cloves, sliced thin

32 littleneck clams, scrubbed
and rinsed

1 cup white wine

½ cup clam juice

1 cup fresh parsley
leaves, chopped

¼ cup grated
Parmesan cheese

Black pepper, to taste

Vegetarian

As attested by the contents of this book, the protein-packed dishes featuring beef, pork, lamb, chicken, and seafood are the overwhelming favorites for the one-pot chef charged with feeding a family. But that doesn't mean there isn't any room for preparations that eschew meat. With standbys like Ratatouille (see page 217) and deliciously innovative offerings like Squash Risotto (see pages 222–223) and Green Bean & Tofu Casserole (see pages 218–219), going for the green has never been easier, nor more enjoyable.

Veggie Burgers

When you want a break from meat but also crave the great taste and texture of a juicy hamburger, try making these.

1 Place half of the beans, the scallions, and roasted red peppers in a food processor and pulse until the mixture is a thick paste. Transfer to a large bowl.

2 Add the corn, bread crumbs, egg, cilantro, cumin, cayenne, black pepper, and lime juice to the bowl and stir to combine. Add the remaining beans and stir vigorously to get the mixture to hold together. Cover the bowl with plastic wrap and let it sit at room temperature for 30 minutes.

3 Place a 12" cast-iron skillet over medium-high heat and coat the bottom with the olive oil. Form the mixture into four patties. When the oil starts to shimmer, add the patties, cover the skillet, and cook until cooked through, about 5 minutes per side. Serve immediately on hamburger buns with the Guacamole.

INGREDIENTS

1 (14 oz.) can of black beans, drained and rinsed

⅓ cup minced scallions

¼ cup chopped roasted red peppers

¼ cup corn kernels

½ cup bread crumbs

1 egg, lightly beaten

2 tablespoons chopped fresh cilantro

½ teaspoon cumin

½ teaspoon cayenne pepper

½ teaspoon black pepper

1 teaspoon fresh lime juice

1 tablespoon olive oil

Hamburger buns, for serving

Guacamole (see page 28), for serving

Succotash

Switching out the divisive lima bean for protein-rich edamame will make this a welcome sight on any table.

INGREDIENTS

1 cup sliced mushroom caps

1 red onion, minced

4 cups corn kernels (5 ears of corn)

1 red bell pepper, stemmed, seeded, and diced

2 cups fresh or frozen edamame

1 tablespoon unsalted butter

Salt and pepper, to taste

1 tablespoon minced fresh marjoram

½ cup chopped fresh basil

1 Place a 12" cast-iron skillet over medium heat, add the mushrooms and cook until they release their liquid and start to brown, about 10 minutes. Reduce heat to low and cook until the mushrooms are a deep brown, about 15 minutes.

2 Add the onion, raise the heat to medium-high, and cook until it has softened, about 5 minutes. Add the corn, bell pepper, and edamame and cook, stirring frequently, until the corn is tender and bright yellow, about 4 minutes.

3 Add the butter and stir until it has melted and coated all of the vegetables. Season with salt and pepper, add the marjoram and basil, stir to incorporate, and serve.

Ratatouille

YIELD: 4 SERVINGS • ACTIVE TIME: 40 MINUTES
TOTAL TIME: 2 HOURS

Some people think sausage is an essential ingredient, but when your garden is at its peak, this dish has enough flavor to carry on without it.

1 Place a 12" cast-iron skillet over medium-high heat and add half of the olive oil. When the oil starts to shimmer, add the garlic and eggplant and cook, while stirring, until pieces are coated with oil and just starting to sizzle, about 2 minutes.

2 Reduce the heat to medium, add the zucchini, peppers, and remaining oil, and stir to combine. Cover the skillet and cook, while stirring occasionally, until the eggplant, zucchini, and peppers are almost tender, about 15 minutes.

3 Add the tomatoes, stir to combine, and cook until the eggplant, zucchini, and peppers are tender and the tomatoes are wilted, about 25 minutes. Remove the skillet from heat, season with salt and pepper, and allow to sit for at least 1 hour. Reheat before serving.

INGREDIENTS

⅓ cup olive oil

6 garlic cloves, minced

1 eggplant, cut into bite-sized cubes

2 zucchini, sliced into half-moons

2 bell peppers, stemmed, seeded, and diced

4 tomatoes, chopped and seeded

Salt and pepper, to taste

Green Bean & Tofu Casserole

YIELD: 4 SERVINGS • ACTIVE TIME: 5 MINUTES
TOTAL TIME: 2 DAYS

Slow roasting is the key here, as it concentrates everything the tofu soaked up while marinating.

1 To prepare the marinade, place all of the ingredients in a small bowl and stir to combine. Place the marinade and the tofu in a resealable plastic bag, place it in the refrigerator, and let marinate for 2 days.

2 To prepare the casserole, preheat the oven to 375°F. Remove the cubes of tofu from the bag. Place the green beans, mushrooms, sesame oil, and soy sauce in the bag and shake until the vegetables are coated.

3 Line a 9 x 13-inch baking pan with parchment paper and place the tofu on it in an even layer. Place in the oven and roast for 35 minutes. Remove the pan, flip the cubes of tofu over, and push them to the pan's outer edge. Add the green bean-and-mushroom mixture, return the dish to the oven, and roast for 15 minutes, or until the green beans are cooked to your preference. Remove the pan from the oven, garnish with the sesame seeds, and serve.

INGREDIENTS

For the Marinade

3 tablespoons soy sauce

2 tablespoons rice vinegar

1 tablespoon sesame oil

1 tablespoon honey

Pinch of cinnamon

Pinch of black pepper

For the Casserole

1 (14 oz.) package of extra-firm tofu, drained and cut into 1" cubes

1 lb. green beans

4 oz. shiitake mushrooms, sliced

2 tablespoons sesame oil

1 tablespoon soy sauce

For Garnish

2 tablespoons sesame seeds

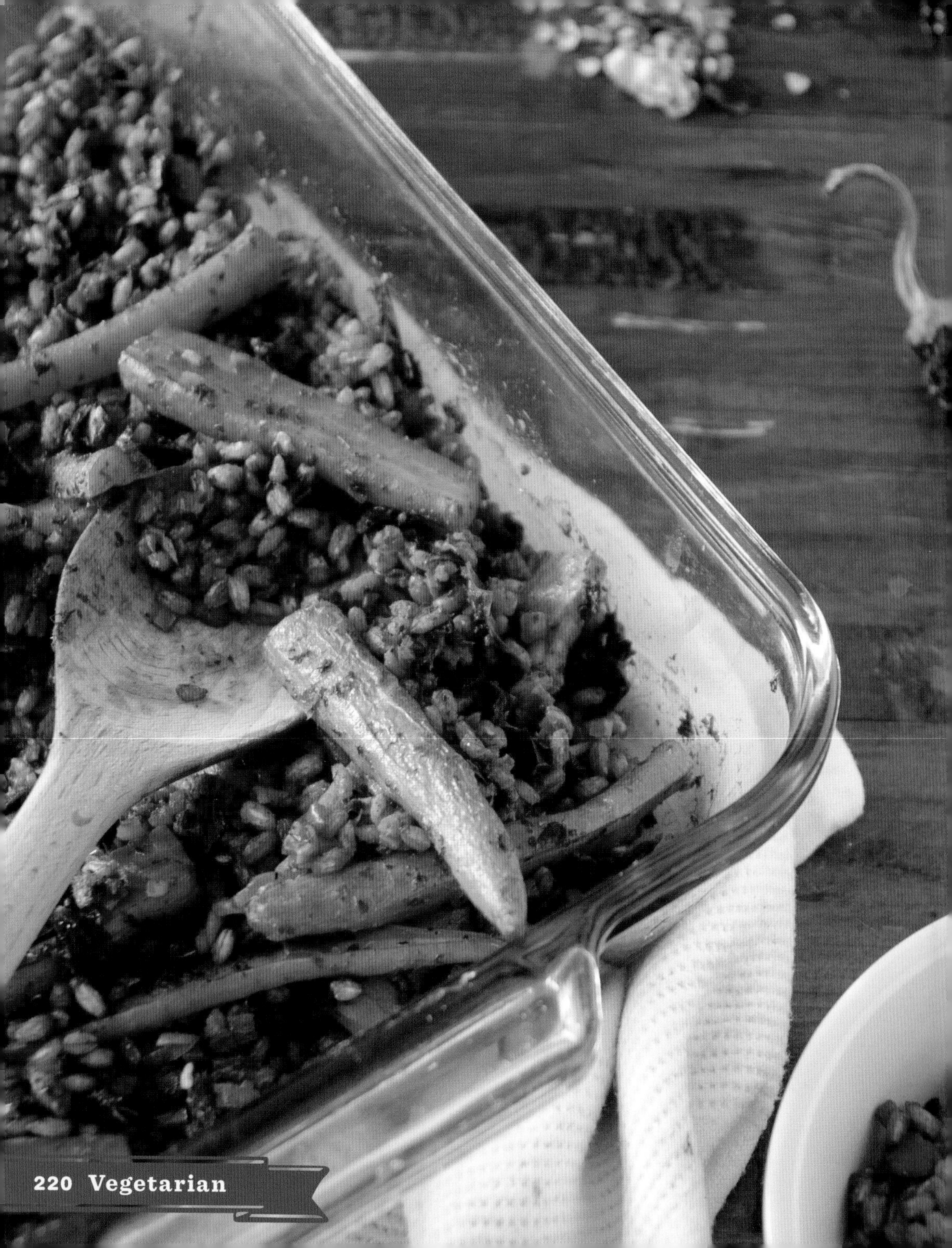

Sweet & Spicy Roasted Barley

**YIELD: 4 SERVINGS • ACTIVE TIME: 20 MINUTES
TOTAL TIME: 1½ HOURS**

This dish is light, sweet, spicy, and nutty. Considering how affordable all of the ingredients are, that's whole a lot of flavor for not very much money.

1 Preheat the oven to 375°F. Place the carrots in a 9 x 13-inch baking pan, drizzle with olive oil, and season with salt and pepper. Place in the oven and roast until the carrots are slightly soft to the touch, about 45 minutes.

2 While the carrots are cooking, open the Pasilla peppers and discard the seeds and stems. Place the peppers in a bowl, add the boiling water, and cover the bowl with aluminum foil.

3 When the carrots are cooked, remove the pan from the oven and add the remaining ingredients and the liquid the peppers have been soaking in. Chop the reconstituted peppers, add them to the pan, and spread the mixture out so that the liquid is covering the barley. Cover the pan tightly with aluminum foil, place it in the oven, and bake until the barley is tender, about 45 minutes. Fluff with a fork and serve immediately.

INGREDIENTS

5 carrots, peeled and cut into 3" pieces

Olive oil, to taste

Salt and pepper, to taste

6 dried Pasilla peppers

2¼ cups boiling water

1 cup pearl barley

1 red onion, minced

2 tablespoons adobo seasoning

1 tablespoon sugar

1 tablespoon chili powder

¼ cup dried oregano

Squash Risotto

YIELD: 6 SERVINGS • ACTIVE TIME: 40 MINUTES
TOTAL TIME: 1 HOUR

Risotto is so much more than a bowl of rice, particularly when you add the famed sweetness of butternut squash.

1 Place 2 tablespoons of the butter in a Dutch oven and melt over medium heat. Add half of the onions and cook until translucent. Add the squash, the tablespoon of salt, and the milk, reduce the heat to low, and cook until the squash is tender, about 20 minutes. Strain, discard the cooking liquid, and transfer the squash and onions to a blender. Puree until smooth and then set aside.

2 Wipe out the Dutch oven and add the stock. Bring to a boil, transfer to a heatproof bowl, and set aside.

3 Place the remaining butter in the Dutch oven and melt over medium heat. Add the remaining onions and cook until translucent, about 3 minutes. Add the

rice and remaining salt and cook, while stirring constantly, until you can smell a toasted nutty aroma. Be careful not to brown the rice.

4 Deglaze the pan with the white wine and continue to stir until all the liquid has evaporated. Add the stock in 1-cup increments and stir constantly until all of the stock has been absorbed. Add the squash puree and kale, stir to incorporate, and season to taste. Add the walnuts and dried cranberries, stir to incorporate, and serve.

1 stick unsalted butter

3 cups diced onions

1 small butternut squash, peeled and diced

1 tablespoon kosher salt, plus 2 teaspoons

3 cups whole milk

5 cups Vegetable Stock (see page 16)

2 cups arborio rice

2 cups white wine

3 cups baby kale, stems removed, leaves chopped

¾ cup toasted walnuts

½ cup dried cranberries

Spinach & Mushroom Quinoa

**YIELD: 6 SERVINGS • ACTIVE TIME: 20 MINUTES
TOTAL TIME: 5 HOURS**

Folding in the herbs at the end of your preparation packs this dish with tons of fresh flavor.

1 Place all of the ingredients, except for the spinach and fresh herbs, in a slow cooker and cook on high until the quinoa is slightly fluffy, about 4 hours.

2 Add the spinach and turn off the heat. Keep the slow cooker covered and let sit for 1 hour.

3 Fluff the quinoa with a fork, add the basil, dill, and thyme, and fold to incorporate. Season with salt and pepper and serve.

INGREDIENTS

1½ cups quinoa, rinsed

2½ cups Vegetable Stock (see page 16)

1 yellow onion, diced

½ red bell pepper, stemmed, seeded, and diced

¾ lb. baby portobello mushrooms, chopped

2 garlic cloves, minced

1 tablespoon kosher salt, plus more to taste

1 tablespoon black pepper, plus more to taste

3 cups baby spinach

1½ cups chopped fresh basil

¼ cup chopped fresh dill

2 tablespoons fresh thyme leaves, minced

Veggie Lo Mein

YIELD: 6 SERVINGS • ACTIVE TIME: 15 MINUTES TOTAL TIME: 30 MINUTES

This dish works either hot or cold, making it a perfect option for summertime, when a hot meal can be the last thing you want.

INGREDIENTS

¼ cup sesame oil

3 tablespoons soy sauce

2 tablespoons black vinegar

1 tablespoon brown sugar

3 tablespoons fish sauce

1 tablespoon olive oil

6 scallions, whites minced, greens cut into 2" pieces

1 tablespoon minced ginger

2 garlic cloves, minced

4 oz. button mushrooms, sliced

½ white onion, sliced

½ cup bean sprouts

1 carrot, peeled and cut into matchsticks

2 lbs. lo mein noodles

1 Place the sesame oil, soy sauce, black vinegar, brown sugar, and fish sauce in a mixing bowl, stir to combine, and set the dressing aside.

2 Place the olive oil, scallion whites, ginger, and garlic in a Dutch oven and cook over high heat for 2 minutes. Add the mushrooms, onion, bean sprouts, and carrot and cook until the vegetables are cooked but still crisp, about 4 minutes. Remove the mixture from the pan and set aside to cool.

3 Wipe out the pot, fill it with water, and bring to a boil. Add the noodles and cook until al dente, about 6 minutes. Drain and add the noodles to the mixing bowl containing the dressing. Toss to coat and add the vegetables and the scallion greens. Serve immediately or refrigerate for up to 2 days.

INGREDIENTS

Salt, to taste

1 lb. elbow macaroni

7 tablespoons unsalted butter

2 cups panko bread crumbs

½ yellow onion, minced

3 tablespoons
all-purpose flour

1 tablespoon yellow mustard

1 teaspoon turmeric

1 teaspoon granulated garlic

1 teaspoon white pepper

2 cups light cream

2 cups whole milk

1 lb. American cheese, sliced

10 oz. Boursin cheese

½ lb. extra sharp cheddar
cheese, sliced

Mac & Cheese

YIELD: 6 SERVINGS • ACTIVE TIME: 15 MINUTES
TOTAL TIME: 1 HOUR

Even though the cheese in this dish will stick to your ribs, seconds are a must. Reserve it for those nights when you're especially hungry and can afford to relax after the meal.

1 Preheat the oven to 400°F. Fill a Dutch oven with water, add salt to taste, and bring to a boil. Add the macaroni and cook until it is just shy of al dente, about 7 minutes. Drain and set aside.

2 Place the pot over medium heat and add 3 tablespoons of the butter. Cook until the butter starts to give off a nutty smell and brown. Add the bread crumbs, stir, and cook for 4 to 5 minutes, until the bread crumbs start to look like wet sand. Remove from the pan and set aside.

3 Wipe the Dutch oven out with a towel, place over medium-high heat, and add the onion and the remaining butter. Cook, while stirring, until the onion is soft, about 10 minutes. Add the flour and stir to prevent lumps from forming.

Add the mustard, turmeric, granulated garlic, and white pepper and whisk until combined. Add the light cream and the milk and whisk until they have been incorporated. Reduce heat to medium and bring the mixture to a simmer. Once you start to see small bubbles forming around the outside of the mixture, add the cheeses one at a time, stirring to incorporate before adding the next one. When the cheeses have been incorporated and the mixture is smooth, cook until the flour taste is gone, about 10 minutes. Return the macaroni to the pan, stir, and top with the bread crumbs.

4 Place the Dutch oven in the oven and bake until the bread crumbs are crispy, 10 to 15 minutes. Remove from the oven and serve immediately.

Manicotti

YIELD: 6 SERVINGS • ACTIVE TIME: 15 MINUTES
TOTAL TIME: 1 HOUR

By removing the step of boiling the manicotti shells, we give you time to kick back and enjoy a glass of wine.

1 Preheat the oven to 400°F. Place the olive oil in a 12" cast-iron skillet and warm over medium-high heat. When the oil starts to shimmer, add the onion and garlic and cook until the onion is translucent, about 3 minutes. Season with salt and pepper and add the oregano, granulated garlic, granulated onion, and red pepper flakes. Stir to combine, transfer the mixture to a mixing bowl, and let cool.

2 Wipe out the skillet, add the ricotta to the onion-and-garlic mixture, and stir to combine. Add the basil, fold to incorporate, and then fill a piping bag with the mixture. Fill the manicotti shells, place them in the skillet, and top with the Marinara Sauce. Cover the skillet, place it in the oven, and bake until the pasta is al dente and the filling is hot, about 35 minutes.

3 Remove the skillet from the oven and remove the cover. Top with the Parmesan and mozzarella, return to the oven, and bake until the cheeses have melted. Garnish with the parsley and serve immediately.

> **TIP:** IF YOU DO NOT HAVE A PIPING BAG, SIMPLY FILL A RESEALABLE PLASTIC BAG WITH THE RICOTTA MIXTURE AND THEN CUT OFF ONE OF THE BOTTOM CORNERS.

2 tablespoons olive oil

1 yellow onion, diced

4 garlic cloves, minced

Salt and pepper, to taste

1 tablespoon dried oregano

½ tablespoon granulated garlic

½ tablespoon granulated onion

Pinch of red pepper flakes

2 cups ricotta cheese

2 tablespoons chopped fresh basil

15 manicotti shells

4 cups Marinara Sauce (see page 32)

1 cup grated Parmesan cheese

1 cup grated mozzarella cheese

2 tablespoons chopped fresh parsley, for garnish

1 tablespoon kosher salt

3 cups ricotta cheese

2 eggs

1½ cups shredded Italian cheese blend (equal parts Asiago, fontina, mozzarella, provolone, Parmesan, and Romano), plus more for topping

½ teaspoon kosher salt

½ teaspoon black pepper

½ teaspoon onion powder

½ teaspoon garlic powder

Pinch of freshly grated nutmeg

½ tablespoon dried basil

½ tablespoon dried oregano

½ cup chopped fresh parsley

2 cups Marinara Sauce (see page 32), plus more as needed

1 box of no-boil lasagna noodles

Lasagna

YIELD: 6 SERVINGS • ACTIVE TIME: 20 MINUTES
TOTAL TIME: 1 HOUR AND 15 MINUTES

Add some buttery garlic bread and a simple salad and you have an assured crowd-pleaser.

1 Preheat the oven to 350°F. Place all of the ingredients, except for the lasagna noodles, in a large mixing bowl and stir to combine.

2 Cover the bottom of a square 8" baking dish with marinara. Place a layer of lasagna noodles on top and cover them with one-third of the marinara-and-cheese mixture. Alternate layers of the noodles and the mixture until all of the mixture has been used up. Top with another layer of noodles and spread a thin layer of sauce over them.

3 Place the dish in the oven and bake for 45 minutes. Remove from the oven, sprinkle more of the cheese blend on top, and return to the oven. Bake until the cheese has melted, about 5 minutes. Remove from the oven and let stand for 20 minutes before slicing and serving.

Metric Equivalents

Weights

1 ounce	28 grams
2 ounces	57 grams
4 ounces (¼ pound)	113 grams
8 ounces (½ pound)	227 grams
16 ounces (1 pound)	454 grams

Volume Measures

⅛ teaspoon		0.6 ml
¼ teaspoon		1.23 ml
½ teaspoon		2.5 ml
1 teaspoon		5 ml
1 tablespoon (3 teaspoons)	½ fluid ounce	15 ml
2 tablespoons	1 fluid ounce	29.5 ml
¼ cup (4 tablespoons)	2 fluid ounces	59 ml
⅓ cup (5⅓ tablespoons)	2.7 fluid ounces	80 ml
½ cup (8 tablespoons)	4 fluid ounces	120 ml
⅔ cup (10⅔ tablespoons)	5.4 fluid ounces	160 ml
¾ cup (12 tablespoons)	6 fluid ounces	180 ml
1 cup (16 tablespoons)	8 fluid ounces	240 ml

Temperature Equivalents

°F	°C	Gas Mark
225	110	¼
250	130	½
275	140	1
300	150	2
325	170	3
350	180	4
375	190	5
400	200	6
425	220	7
450	230	8
475	240	9
500	250	10

Length Measures

¹⁄₁₆-inch	1.6 mm
⅛-inch	3 mm
¼-inch	0.63 cm
½-inch	1.25 cm
¾-inch	2 cm
1-inch	2.5 cm

Index

ABOUT CIDER MILL PRESS BOOK PUBLISHERS

Good ideas ripen with time. From seed to harvest, Cider Mill Press brings fine reading, information, and entertainment together between the covers of its creatively crafted books. Our Cider Mill bears fruit twice a year, publishing a new crop of titles each spring and fall.

"Where Good Books Are Ready for Press"

Visit us online at
cidermillpress.com
or write to us at
PO Box 454
12 Spring St.
Kennebunkport, Maine 04046